THIRTY-TWO PATHS OF WISDOM

ORDO · ASTRI

THIRTY-TWO PATHS

OF

WISDOM

KEY TO THE HERMETIC QABALAH:
COMMENTARY ON THE SHINING PATHS
OF THE SEPHER YETZIRAH
AND THE PATHS OF EVIL

OLIVER ST. JOHN

Thirty-two paths of Wisdom

Key to the Hermetic Qabalah: Commentary on the Shining Paths of the Sepher Yetzirah and the Paths of Evil

ISBN 978-1-0682715-1-9

Paperback edition (June 2025)

ORDO ASTRI IMPRIMATUR

www.ordoastri.org

Our grateful thanks to Steffi Grant, and to Michael Staley of Starfire Publishing Ltd, who kindly gave us the permission to quote at length from Kenneth Grant's book, *The Nightside of Eden*, concerning the inverse aspects of the paths. We also thank Michael Staley for his assistance with ensuring that the quoted passages agree with the revised 2014 edition of the book.

It is written:

As for the likeness of the living creatures, their appearance was like burning coals of fire, and like the appearance of lamps: it went up and down among the living creatures; and the fire was bright, and out of the fire went forth lightning.

And the living creatures ran and returned as the appearance of a flash of lightning.

Ezekiel 1: 13–14

CONTENTS

Preface

Sophia is our Guiding Light.

This book came about primarily from a pressing need to rewrite the commentary on the *Thirty-two paths of Wisdom* from the *Sepher Yetzirah* that appeared in the *Flaming Sword* and some other books. As soon as that work was begun it became evident that it would not in be enough to simply tidy up and clarify the old commentary, removing what had been taken from sources that we now know are not in any way reliable. The occultists of the so-called Western Tradition—which is more of a 'lost tradition' than anything else—have wrested knowledge from ancient traditions and sought to make 'systems' for ready application in the popular magical domain, divorcing that knowledge from its principles and rendering it as mere 'information'. This has been done from a place completely *outside* of those traditions, even when the writers claim or otherwise insinuate to be in the possession of 'initiated secrets'.

A Qabalah by now exists, therefore, that is nothing other than a more or less arbitrary system of correspondences, and that bears no relation to what the Qabalah really is or was—an initiatic, handed on tradition first written down almost two thousand years ago. We are ourselves as much to blame for this as any other, but we can at least, while there is still time, make some reparations.

In this way, occultists are much comparable to the Rabbi Acher in a story from the Talmud that we will later investigate in more detail: on approaching the upper worlds through the means of the 'divine chariot' (*merkebah*), Acher busied himself with cutting off the shoots from the saplings in the garden of Eden, thus removing the fruits of the Tree of Knowledge from their principle hidden in the roots of the Tree of Life. Acher typifies the dissident, 'the one that goes astray', as indicated by his Hebrew name. Acher who, following this 'fall', was no longer the man he was, later related to another Rabbi that a broken vessel of gold or glass can be melted down and made into a new vessel—though he was as yet unable to discern a difference between gold and glass, between the pure metal and the mere artifice. Without the necessary discrimination, no vessel can be made anew, for the old errors will only be repeated.

i

The authorship and the date of origin of the *Sepher Yetzirah* is unknown, a matter that concerns scholars and so the book is often attributed to various names and speculative dates. Scholars cannot understand at all that a written work might not be due to someone's personal invention, whereas traditional knowledge is always handed down. So far as initiation is involved, it is transmitted—which is very nearly the meaning of the word Qabalah. The book is now thought to date from around the first or second century.

The title of the book is usually translated the *Book of Formation*, and while some argue that this is not accurate, what they come up with as an alternative is even less likely and only shows their own predisposition, as we might expect. We will use the word 'Formation' as that clearly relates to a cosmology, which is what this book is at least on the surface; a cosmology can only be understood through the means of form. It must be understood however that ancient doctrines are not concerned with measuring the universe; they are concerned with the subtle worlds of manifestation. The word *Yetzirah* in the Qabalah is descriptive of the whole subtle realm both macrocosmic and microcosmic—by which is meant that which pertains strictly to the human scale. While the *Book of Formation* is often thought to be limited to a cosmological schema, and is frequently described as a 'system'—something that only properly applies to modernity since about the eighteenth century—there is no reason to assume that the texts do not allude to metaphysical or absolute reality. Metaphysics, in the way that we intend to use the term, is not a mere 'abstraction' but is true knowledge and a most exact science that is not in any way comparable to the conventional modern science, which is theoretical knowledge only.

Translators and commentators on sacred texts are often limited to a vaguely understood theological interpretation; they will insist on translating 'creation' everywhere, for example, even when that word, which assumes an anthropomorphic notion of God, does not appear in the sacred language. Likewise, commentators, whether scholarly or otherwise, will always refer to that which is not the product of discursive thought as 'mystical'; yet mysticism is, properly speaking, quite exclusive to the Christian religion.[1]

---

[1] Mysticism is descriptive of emotional psychism and the knowledge that supports it goes no further than theology. It is most often the case that what is called 'mysticism' is not that. Jacob Boehme is nearly always described as a 'Christian mystic' yet he was in reality a Christian hermeticist. Even the work of Eastern sages like Shankaracharya is called 'mystical' by the English translators and apologists.

We therefore use the word 'creation' if that was the word given by the translators, but we do not use it in our commentary. We interpret the meanings in a way that is 'principial', and which we believe accords with the intention of those who wrote down the book in the first place.[2] To assist with accuracy, we sometimes use Sanskrit terms from the Vedanta by way of comparison.

According to some sources, the book was written down by a Neo-Pythagorean some time between the third and sixth centuries, and there is even in it a Gnostic influence.[3] According to A. E. Waite, who translated the book into English, it was introduced to the Christian world via Latin in 1562. The older sections of the *Book of Formation* are indicative of an Alexandrian or an Egyptian Hermetic influence. There are geometric references, for example; geometry is not a part of the earlier Hebraic tradition, especially in the particular way that the Pythagoreans developed it. The main focus of the present work is the text called *Thirty-two paths of Wisdom*, which is thought to have been added to the *Book of Formation* at a much later date than the first sections, which we suppose to have been written down from the oral tradition around the first or second century. The text of the *Thirty-two paths* is certainly written in a different style and seems further removed from all that which characterises the first written down from the oral tradition, and which includes much deliberate use of repetition.

The translations of the verses we use here are from Waite, unless from Westcott, as indicated. Where the language used in the original English translation is awkward or obfuscating, we have paraphrased it instead of quoting it. In some cases, as with the thirteenth path, both Waite and Westcott seem to have been afflicted with almost total incoherence, so we have restructured the translation.

The many considerations involved in a work of this nature can easily lead us away from the living spirit of the *Book of Formation*, one of the most important of Qabalistic source texts. The Hebraic tradition has for many centuries been a closed one, and quite rightly so, but owing to the conditions of the present time, this, and indeed all other ancient traditions, are no longer closed to those who seek knowledge with a pure heart and in good faith. That does exclude those who will seek only some practical or magical *use* of knowledge, and who join others in the mad scramble to get something they want as quickly as possible and with the least effort on their behalf.

---

[2] That is to say, as depending from the highest principle.
[3] Gershom Gerhard Scholem, *Origins of the Kabbalah*, p. 78.

For the latter, this knowledge will remain a closed book forever. How best then to use this book? As with the *Book of Formation* itself, it is best to read the texts aloud, either to yourself or, if you are so fortunate, then to a friend or spouse that has good faith. The texts were also designed for formal meditation, as is shown by this passage from the *Book of Formation*, I: 8:

> Ten ineffable sephiroth: close thy mouth lest it speak and thy heart lest it think; and if thy mouth openeth for utterance and thy heart turneth toward thought, bring them back to thy control. Then here it is, as it is written: 'And the living creatures ran and returned' (Ezekiel 1: 14).

The above accords with the instructions given in the Vedanta, that in meditation one should keep the thoughts in the 'heart' and not pay attention to them, while the breath should be directed upward to the crown (or Kether). The out-breath and the in-breath are analogous with the manifestation of the Cosmos and its withdrawal in *pralaya* (dissolution). Thus, 'And the living creatures ran and returned'.

The first section of this book serves as an introduction to the Qabalah inclusive of the Hebraic tradition, from which the latter was developed, as well as the modern Hermetic tradition with its systems of correspondences. There follows a commentary on the *Thirty-two paths of Wisdom* from the *Book of Formation*. 'The Paths of Evil' concerns the traditional Qliphoth of the first ten paths and those corresponding to the Zodiac. The last section, 'The Tunnels of Set', is a critical reappraisal of Kenneth Grant's *Nightside of Eden*, Part Two, revealing how Aleister Crowley and then Grant and others worked to invert symbolism, effectively removing all spiritual possibilities for those that would follow them. By placing this in the context of the neo-spiritualist and postmodern occult movement, we wish to show how the decline and intellectual collapse of an entire civilisation towards the final dissolution of our world is being supernaturally accelerated.

Sophia be-with-us forever.

Oliver St. John

St. Ives Cornwall Sol in ♈ Luna in ♌ April 2023

The Hebraic Tradition

The books of the Hebrew Talmud ('knowledge') exist in a Babylonian and a Jerusalem version. The Talmud has two main branches of which the first is the Mishnah (משנה), thought to have been written around the second century. This comprises a written compendium of the Oral Torah. The second and later branch is the Gemara (גמרה), thought to have been written down in the fifth century. This is an elucidation of the Mishnah and related writings of the sages.

According to this authority, the Gemara expounds on matters concerning the 'divine chariot' (*merkebah*).[4] A rabbi and his student are riding on donkeys. The student asked the teacher, My teacher, teach me one chapter in the design of the divine chariot. The teacher replied, Have I not taught you: That one may not expound the design of the divine chariot to any person, unless he happens to be a sage who understands on his own accord? Then the student said, My teacher, allow me to say before you one thing that you taught me. That is to say, he respectfully requested to recite before him his own understanding of this.

The teacher then said to him: Speak. And he alighted from the donkey, wrapping his head in his cloak in a manner of reverence, and sat on a stone under an olive tree. The student asked: My teacher, for what reason did you alight from the donkey? The teacher replied: Is it possible that while you are expounding the design of the divine chariot, and the divine presence [Shekinah] should be among us, and the ministering angels are accompanying us, that I should ride on a donkey?

The student began to expound on the design of the divine chariot and fire descended from heaven and encircled all the trees in the field; and the trees began to sing songs of praise to the Lord. An angel also spoke out of the fire, saying: This is the very design of the divine chariot, just as you expounded.

The rabbi then kissed his student on the head and blessed him, for he knew how to expound the design of the divine chariot. He said to him: There are some who expound the Torah's verses well but do not fulfill its imperatives well, and then there are some who fulfill its imperatives well but do not expound its verses well, whereas you expound its verses well and fulfill its imperatives well.

---

[4] Hagigah (*chagigah*) 14b.

The Gemara goes on to tell how this story was repeated before a rabbi and a priest, and they also expounded on the design of the divine chariot. It was on the day of the summer solstice, when there are no clouds in the sky. Yet the heavens became filled with clouds, and there was the appearance of a kind of rainbow in a cloud. And ministering angels gathered and came to listen, like people gathering and coming to see the rejoicing of a bridegroom and bride.

The Rabbi Yochanab ben Zakkai then said to the priest: Happy are all of you, and happy are the mothers who gave birth to you; happy are my eyes that saw this, students such as these. As for you and I, I saw in my dream that we were seated at Mount Sinai, and a divine voice came to us from heaven: Ascend here, ascend here, for large halls [teraklin] and pleasant couches are made up for you. You, your students, and the students of your students are invited to the third group, those who will merit to welcome the divine presence.

There follows a lengthy consideration on the matter of selection, of those who are permitted to go further to the Holy of Holies. The Gemara then continues. The Sages taught: Four entered the orchard [pardes], that is, they dealt with the loftiest secrets of the Torah. They were Ben Azzai, ben Zoma, ben Acher, and Rabbi Akiva. Rabbi Akiva, the senior among them, said to them: When, upon your arrival in the upper worlds, you reach pure marble stones, do not say: Water, water, although they appear to be water, because it is stated: 'He who speaks falsehood shall not be established before My eyes' (book of Psalms 101: 7).

The Gemara proceeds to relate what happened to each of them: Ben Azzai glimpsed at the divine presence and died. And with regard to him the verse states: 'Precious in the eyes of the Lord is the death of His pious ones' (Psalms 116: 15). That is to say, he went straight to heaven. Ben Zoma glimpsed at the divine presence and was injured, that is to say, he lost his mind. With regard to him the verse states: 'Have you found honey? Eat as much as is sufficient for you, lest you become sick' (Proverbs 25: 16). Acher chopped down the shoots of saplings. In other words, he became a heretic, not knowing the divine principle. Only Rabbi Akiva came out safely.

The name Zoma means 'thought', and it is recounted how the Rabbi was able to construe very obscure matters of doctrine, but was not yet prepared for the higher truth. As for Acher, who chopped down saplings, the verse states: 'Do not let your mouth bring your flesh into guilt' (Ecclesiastes 5: 5).

2

What was it that led Acher to heresy? He saw the angel Metatron, who said: There is a tradition that in the upper worlds no one sits down; there is no idleness. No one competes with another here, and one must always face the divine presence, never turning their back. Seeing that someone other than the Lord Himself was seated above, Acher thought there might be two authorities, and even another that controls the world in addition to God. These thoughts led Acher to heresy. He fell prey to dualism. The name Acher means 'astray', for he went astray, and was no longer the man that he was.

But all was not lost (there are many stories of Rabbi Acher). Later he said, after going astray, Even as golden vessels and glass vessels have a remedy when they have broken, as they can be melted down and made into new vessels, so too a Torah scholar, although he has transgressed, has a remedy. And the Rabbi Meir said to him: If so, you too, can return from your ways.

Our modern Hermetic Qabalah, developed from a place outside of any tradition, makes much use of the method alluded to above, called the 'divine chariot'. In its systematised form it has become known as 'rising on the planes', though that is often done in a way that owes to more or less artificial correspondences, and is removed entirely from the traditional knowledge and spirit. If we are going to work with the Qabalah in any shape or form, we should at least know something of the tradition. It is also important to understand how easy it is to fool ourselves with the modern 'visualisation' techniques and symbolism, even when that is combined with meditation, so that we think we are obtaining cosmic visions and the like, or that we are even entering the Holy of Holies when in fact we have gone no further than our own vain imagining. The tale of the three students and their teacher illustrates the point very well. These did not pass all the way to the summit of the Tree of Life; they stopped short at the threshold of the abode of the Shekinah or Holy Presence.[5] The Shekinah nonetheless was able to visit them, as evidenced by the cloud and the rainbow, her symbols. One of the men was struck dead—though he seems to have obtained the supreme liberation (Sanskrit *moksha*). The second lost his mind (or reason). The third received nothing, because he was far too eager to grasp at knowledge so that it would serve *him*. Even though the Archangel Metatron spoke to him direct, all that did was confuse him, so that he 'went astray', as indicated by his name.

---

[5] It should be noted that Kabbalists within the Hebraic tradition make use of a complex Tree of Life that incorporates all the four worlds, whereas we usually compact the Tree into one that includes all of them.

So let us not kid ourselves that we are entering upon holy ground when all we are doing is playing pin the tail on the donkey. In today's world, where hyperbole is the usual mode of expression for the most ordinary things imaginable, modern 'magicians' will claim that they are experiencing 'revelations' or are on the edge of inexpressible truths. If the gates of heaven were truly opened, we would not then go on to continue with mundane preoccupations as though nothing had happened at all, or with temporary excitement of the senses, as though we had seen an entertaining play or movie or experienced a curious dream. Real initiation—and that is after all what this is all about—changes the state of the being permanently and forever.

The Sepher Yetzirah

Our interest here is limited for the most part to the *Book of Formation* and the Qabalah that is a particular development or adaptation of the ancient Hebraic *Etz Chaim* or Tree of Life. Even more specifically, the intention of this book is to make a commentary on the *Thirty-two paths of Wisdom*, which is included among the texts of the Book of Formation though it is thought to have been written at a later date than the chapters that are obviously from the oral tradition. Regarding the Tree of Life, from the book of *Etz Chaim*,

> Before the archetypes [principles] were designated [made subject to determination] and the creatures created [produced] there was simple [or rather primordial] supernal light filling all existence [though this cannot properly be called 'existence' as we are not yet dealing here with manifestation]. There was no emptiness or free space or air cavity, rather everything was full with that infinite, simple [primordial] light which has no beginning or ending. Everything was that single, equal simple [primordial] light that we refer to as Ain Soph Aur, the Infinite Light.[6]

To paraphrase the rest of this passage: There then arose in this simple or primordial desire the will to manifest the worlds of being, to set up the archetypes, principles or sephiroth and bring forth into the light divine perfection, names and powers. Therein, it is said, is the reason for the creation of all worlds. And furthermore, God then constricted or *concentrated* His infinite Self into the centre point in His Self in the absolute middle of His Light.

אין סוף אור

The three veils upon the infinite, the Ain Soph Aur, as preceding or acting as the higher unmanifest principle before the emanations or sephiroth of the Tree of Life, is familiar to those who have studied and practiced the Hermetic Qabalah. The 'constriction' or perhaps better, *concentration* to a single 'point' is only understood through meditation, where this 'act of God' is replicated in all traditions. The mind is concentrated (Sanskrit *dharana*) so that a flow of knowledge (*dhyana*) comes forth.

---

[6] Translation J. Hershy Worch, *Sefer Yetzirah and Commentary* 2007. Our commentary or clarification of the text is in parantheses.

The contraction and the 'point' is analogous as the metaphysical principle Itself is not within time and space and has no dimension, whether great or small—yet It may be symbolised as either of these. The manifestation, called Maya in Sanskrit, comes about through the sheer 'presence' of the primordial infinite light. Even Maya, second to the 'first cause' of all manifestation, is inexplicable, having neither beginning nor end. It can only be known through direct knowledge of God and the absolute, called *jnana* in Sanskrit and *gnosis* in Greek.

Now, to make clear what was said earlier regarding the scholarly confusion that abounds through incomprehension of metaphysics, we will quote briefly from one translator of the *Book of Formation* that has produced a lengthy commentary.[7] He sees a contradiction where no such contradiction exists:

> Whoever examines the words of Rabbi Isaac Luria, the Ari [the lion], can see an obvious and glaring contradiction in his words. On the one hand he says, 'everything was full with that infinite, simple light which has no beginning or ending. Everything was that single, equal simple light'. While on the other hand he says, 'Then God constricted His infinite Self into the centre point in His Self in the absolute centre of His Light.' The difficulty is self-explanatory; if there is no beginning or ending in the infinite, how are we to imagine or think of a middle and centre point?

The translator's subsequent attempts to 'explain' this only lead us further and further away from the meaning of the text. He decides that what he terms 'simple desire' must be the same as the most basic desire that any human or animal might 'feel in their gut'. All of this, which only gets worse as he plunges into psychological and even scientific analogies, owes to a 'simple' anthropomorphisation of God or the divine absolute that rests on theology, not metaphysics.[8] There is no need to spend too much time on this, so let it suffice to say that the 'middle and centre point' *is* the infinite, regarded from another perspective. It is called a 'centre' and a 'middle', but it is not within manifestation and so is not in any way 'located' in time or space. The Ain Soph Aur is *already concentrated*—this is not descriptive of a sequence of 'events' taking place one after the other.

---

[7] Worch [*ibid*].

[8] In another place, the translator thinks that the 'lightning flash' is described in particular language so as to convey a 'blast from an oven', which he then likens to an 'impression left on the retina', thus reducing the symbolism to a physical explanation that has nothing to do with the real meaning and only gives rise to further and more pointless speculation.

The symbolism of the lightning or thunder flash is used in more than one tradition to express simultaneity. The first chapter of the *Book of Formation* concerns the 'ten ineffable sephiroth':

Ten ineffable sephiroth: their appearance is like that of a flash of lightning, their goal is infinite. His word is in them when they emanate and when they return; at His bidding do they haste like a whirlwind; and before His throne do they prostrate themselves.

Ten ineffable sephiroth: their end is in their beginning and likewise their beginning is in their end, as the flame is bound to the burning coal. The Lord is one and the Formator is one [with Him] and hath no second: what number canst thou count before one?

This has remarkable resonance with the Hindu doctrine of cosmic cycles, where the entire manifestation of the worlds is likened to an out-breath, and the withdrawal of those worlds at the end of time in the *mahapralaya* ('great dissolution') is as an in-breath. The Lord that 'hath no second' is directly equivalent even to the Advaitan 'One without a second' that is ascribed to the supreme Brahma.

א מ ש

The book goes on to explain how from the throne of the Spirit of the Living Elohim (אלהים), the 'voice, spirit and word of the Holy One', also described previously as the 'Formator', is produced the three principles or Mother letters: Aleph (א), Mem (מ) and Shin (ש). These have a correspondence with Air, Water and Fire. The Elohim as the 'Formator'—this is the *Book of Formation* so it could also have been called the *Book of Elohim*—is similar to the principle of Maya, who produces from out of her own essence all the manifest worlds and creatures, and is not truly separate from Brahma.

Air from Spirit : Water from Air : Fire from Water

From Air is formed the twenty-two basal letters. By Water these are bound or 'plaited', or 'hewed together as a wall', or 'covered as a building'. The Elohim cover them with snow, and from this the earth is brought forth. In the Hindu tradition, the world egg breaks into two pieces, and from the top half, which is golden, is formed heaven, which covers, and from the lower half, which is silver, is formed the earth, which supports. The silver colour, as with the whiteness of snow, is linked to the mountains of the earth as opposed to the seas.

From Fire is formed the Throne of Glory, and from there proceed the seraphim and ophanim, all the angels and powers, which are in reality the attributes of the divine in manifestation. And these are called His dwelling, which refers to the Shekinah or holy presence.

What follows is important, for from the twenty-two basal letters are chosen three that have a 'secret belonging to the three mothers' Aleph, Mem and Shin. The three letters IHV are then put within the Great Name and are 'sealed with six extensions', which is achieved through the six permutations of the three letters.[9] There is then a replication, to a certain extent, of what was described with the Ain Soph Aur in the book of *Etz Chaim*, where there is a 'concentration' of the infinite that makes manifestation possible.[10] At the Yetziratic level, the concentration is identical with what is otherwise called the three-dimensional cross or the Cube of Space. This is composed of a vertical and horizontal line, which becomes three-dimensional when another line passes through the centre at right angles to the others.

> The symbolism can be understood, through the analogy of the weave of warp and weft, as depicting a universal cross that is able to replicate indefinitely, producing numerous worlds or states of being as well as countless individual creatures, which are a microcosmic reflection of the macrocosm.[11]

The way this is described in the *Book of Formation* is suggestive of a ritual that forms the Cube (or sphere) of Space, and which is identical to the Hindu *namashka*, 'naming the space' that is done before and after any sacred dance—as we shall now see.

---

[9] The Great Name is the Tetragrammaton IHVH. This name of God is never pronounced or vocalised in the Hebraic tradition. It is written and can be read with the eyes, mind and heart, but is never spoken with the mouth.

[10] There are four worlds of the Qabalah: Atziluth, Briah, Yetzirah and Assiah. What took place with the infinite was at the level of Atziluth, the 'word of pure emanation', whereas what is described in the Book of Formation is in Yetzirah, the subtle or 'astral' level of manifestation. See *Hermetic Qabalah Foundation—Complete Course*.

[11] *The Way of Knowledge*, p. 69.

The Ritual of the Sepher Yetzirah

Sepher Yetzirah, I: 13

He chose three of the simple letters, a secret belonging to the three mothers, אמש, and put them in His Great Name, and sealed with them six extensions.[12]

He sealed the Height stretched upwards and sealed it with:

יהו

He sealed the Depth stretched downwards and sealed it with:

יוה

He sealed the East stretched forwards and sealed it with:

היו

He sealed the West stretched backwards and sealed it with:

הוי

He sealed the North stretched to the right and sealed it with:

ויה

He sealed the South stretched to the left and sealed it with:

והי

These are the ten ineffable sephiroth: one—the Spirit of the Living Elohim; two—Air from Spirit; three—Water from Air; four—Fire from Water; Height, Depth, East, West, North and South.

---

[12] IHV is equal to 21, a number of Kether and of Tiphereth.

The Hermetic Qabalah

The spelling of the word 'Qabalah' is used to designate the Hermetic Qabalah. When spelled 'Kabbalah', this refers to the Jewish esoteric teachings based on the study of the Torah and other scriptures. 'Cabala' is a form of Christian mysticism influenced by Jewish esotericism during the Renaissance. Both the latter forms are to a large extent considered to be heretical by the orthodoxy.

The word Qabalah (קבלה) signifies the reception of a spiritual influence and, at the same time, the initiatic transmission itself. The Tree of Life provides a basis for ritual and meditation. It consists of a particular development of the traditional teachings. The form of the Tree of Life most widely used today is a diagram of ten discs or numbers (sephiroth) and twenty-two inter-connecting pathways. The philosophical and numerical basis of the Tree of Life is thought to owe more to Pythagoras than it does to Moses; however, scholars tend to see everything as derived from the Greeks but the Hebrew tradition is unique in many respects. Nonetheless, study of the Pythagorean ternary, quaternary and decad does much to provide a more solid basis for an intellectual understanding of the Qabalah.

The Golden Dawn made use of the correspondences to the letters given in the *Book of Formation*, but through systematisation tended to lose sight of the metaphysical basis that is alluded to in that work. Unfortunately, this is still the overriding concern of 'occult scholars', who are comparable to Ben Acher in the Talmudic text, who cut off the plants from their principle. In their attempt to find meaning in the texts, they instead find only baffling contradictions where no such contradictions exist. They rush at the ancient texts, cutting them to pieces with irrelevant analysis and supposition, piling in as many 'learned' references as possible, isolating 'information' from the wisdom and tabulating it into 'systems' of correspondences. This is then supposed to facilitate the ready *application* of knowledge, bypassing the need to understand anything at all!

The *Book of Formation* does not include the sephirotic model of the Tree of Life as used by the modern Hermeticists. There are many variations on how to make the twenty-two Hebrew letters 'fit' the Tree of Life, based on quite differing interpretations of the *Book of Formation* or other texts. Some will even get heated, arguing a case for this and that 'system' to be the correct one. Those who do so know nothing of metaphysics, for tabulated systems and diagrams, while having their use, destroy all metaphysical possibilities.

Our attribution of Hebrew letters to the twenty-two connecting paths here is nonetheless derived from the Golden Dawn, who used the Athanasius Kircher arrangement.[13] The correspondences of the letters to the planets and Zodiac are as worked out (presumably) by Westcott and Mathers. These differ from that which is given in the *Book of Formation*, which is internally consistent—the letters of the planets follow the natural order of the alphabet from *beth* according to the seven days of the week: Sun, Moon, Mars, Mercury, Jupiter, Venus and Saturn. That does not suit our placement of letters and Tarot trumps to the twenty-two paths of the Tree of Life. There are also, it should be noted, different versions of the source codices, which give different correspondences. From Kircher onward, people even added Uranus, Neptune and Pluto.

In the *Book of Formation*, *aleph* corresponds to Air and is the first of a triadic principle. These are not the terrestrial elements; their operation is therefore on a higher plane than that of the classical four elements. Aleph is the principle, the first after Spirit (Elohim), as involved in manifestation. The other two principial or Mother letters are *mem*, corresponding to Water, and *shin*, corresponding to Fire. From these three Mother letters is formed, as we have previously mentioned, the three-dimensional cross of space, giving rise to height, depth and the four directions. All other principles are derived from them. As in other traditions, the letters are understood to be the word of God, and are as the leaves on the Tree of Life, or leaves in a Book of Life. The *Book of Formation* is thus based more upon the six directions of space as within a sphere than any linear diagrammatic model.

Our reason for using the Tree of Life model of ten sephiroth and twenty-two connecting paths and the Golden Dawn attributions of the Tarot is that this is by now conventional and is well known to our readers and students, even if it happens that the Tarot plays no part in the traditional Kabbalah, as distinguished from modern Hermetic Qabalah. Meditation on the thirty-two paths and their meanings has proved the validity of the correspondences included here, and so we make no apology for having presented them as we have done. Our system of correspondences is practical. It enables a ready mnemonic and a means of training the mind as a preparation for liberation from the constriction of the gross concrete mentality that now afflicts our civilisation as we draw to the end of the Kali Yuga.

---

[13] Athanasius Kircher, *Oedipus Aegyptiacus* (published 1652 and 1654).

The Hermetic Tree of Life

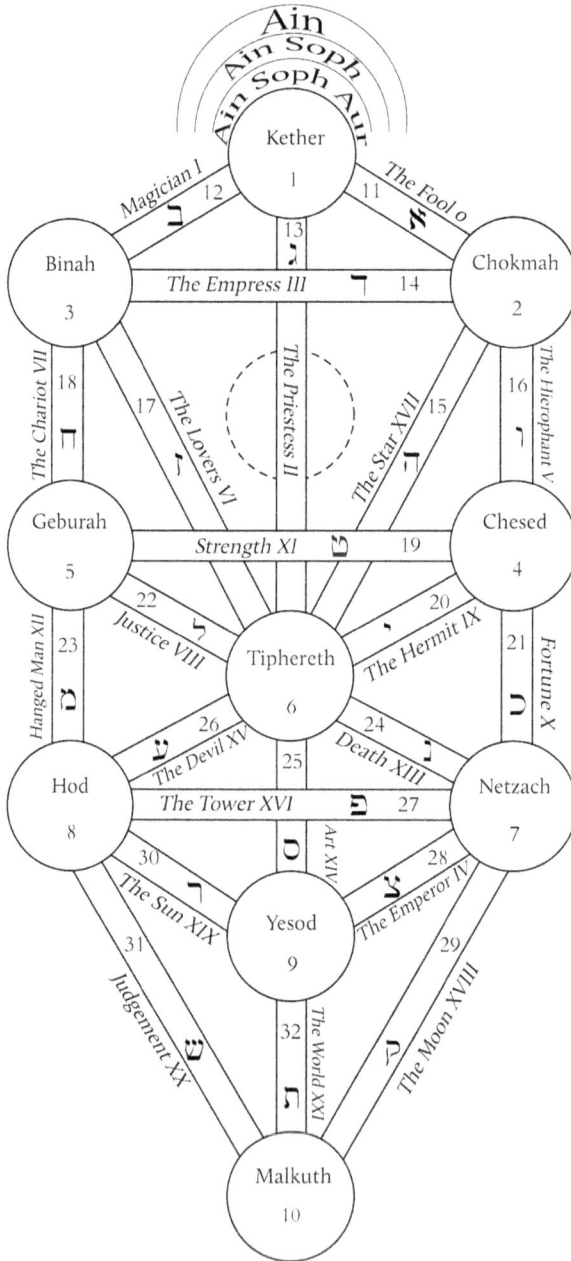

The Hermetic Tree of Life

The Tree of Life represents man and the universe, microcosm and macrocosm. There are three veils upon the Infinite. The first of these is Ain, usually called 'Negativity' but this is only because nothing can be said about the supreme reality, which is free of all determinations.[14] This tends towards the Ain Soph, Limitless. The Ain Soph then precipitates the third negative veil, the Ain Soph Aur, Limitless Light.

The Tree of Life itself reflects the supernal triad, the first three numbers. From the first triad, the perfect expression of metaphysical 'unity', there come forth the intellectual and moral qualities in man, and finally the whole universe of manifestation as it is apprehended by the senses. Between Kether and Malkuth, Alpha and Omega, exist all possible phases of manifestation between spirit and substance.

Sephira, 'number', is singular while *sephiroth* is the plural form. The sephiroth from one to ten represent a 'lightning flash' series of emanations or radiations from the spiritual essence. These combine to form the whole of Creation.[15] The apparent progression of the ten numbers or sephiroth symbolises the divine unfoldment through manifestation. The completion, end result or furthest degree of this is summed up in the tenth sephira, Malkuth, the Kingdom. Malkuth is the domain of phenomena—all of the appearances, objects and things that are discernible to the human sense perceptions. This ordered, symmetrical unfolding through various veils or coverings is the basis of most traditional cosmological teaching.

When a line is drawn from the first to the tenth sephira following the numerical sequence, the figure known as the Lightning Flash or Flaming Sword is created. The Flaming Sword descends the Tree of Life while the Serpent of Wisdom, usually shown as winding upwards around the twenty-two pathways, ascends it. The two currents, the Sword and the Serpent, symbolise the dual powers sustaining the universe.

---

[14] Kircher's translation of the *Sepher Yetzirah* has it that the sephiroth were created 'out of nothing', which owes to his notion of Ain. Unfortunately, this false notion seems to have become established as though it were 'fact'.

[15] By 'creation' we mean that which is produced and therefore determined. Manifestation and being come about by the 'essence' (Sanskrit *purusha*) acting upon 'substance' (*prakriti*). These matters are fully explained in *The Way of Knowledge*.

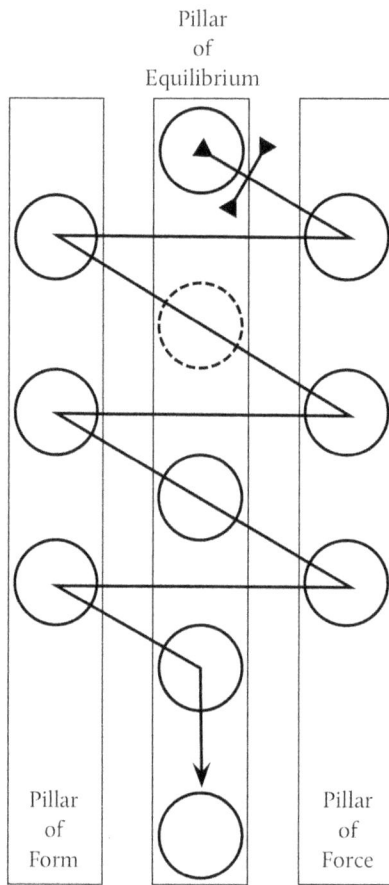

Pillar
of
Equilibrium

Pillar
of
Form

Pillar
of
Force

The descending force tends towards manifestation whereby form and substance become subject to increasing complexity and density through determination.[16] The ascending current is transcendental. By it, consciousness returns from the hell of separation to blissful union, from imprisonment in dark unknowing to the freedom of eternity.

The twenty-two connecting pathways each correspond to one of the letters of the Hebrew alphabet. These are the means of knowing the potencies of the numbers or sephiroth. The sephiroth also have a relation to the chakras. These can be thought of as centres of cosmic power bearing an analogous correspondence to locations in or about the human body.

The Tree of Life manifests within the vertical polarity of the axis of 'spirit' and 'substance' (see diagram on the facing page). The axis is called the middle pillar, or pillar of equilibrium. The Tree of Life also manifests within the horizontal polarity of a force and form duality represented by the two lateral pillars. If we face the symbolic Tree, then to our right stands the white pillar of Force. This joins the three sephiroth Chokmah, Chesed (or Gedulah) and Netzach. To our left is the black pillar of Form. This joins the sephiroth Binah, Geburah and Hod.

Meditation upon the Tree of Life is to produce knowledge of the Reality that is veiled by the symbol; the Qabalah should not therefore be thought of as the play of abstract symbolism alone. The truth of this can be only ascertained by meditative work on the Tree.

---

[16] The concretisation of a thing, however, does not make it 'more real', as some dictionaries suggest—which is a complete reversal of the truth.

THIRTY-TWO PATHS OF WISDOM
OF
WISDOM

The Shining Paths

The Intelligence of Wonder

1. Kether, the first path, is called the Intelligence of Wonder or Admirable Intelligence, and Supreme Crown.[17] It is the light of the Primordial Intelligence. The *Book of Formation* says of this path that it is 'the light that imparts understanding of the beginning [*principle*] that is without beginning, and this also is the First Splendour. No created being can attain to its essence [or *essential reality*]'. As the first from the unmanifest principle, Kether is the equivalent of the Sanskrit Ishwara or Lord of the Universe, and as he is creator or producer of beings, no being can be Ishwara. This is supported by the traditional divine name, which is that word heard by Moses, AHIH AShR AHIH, 'I Am That I Am', or more accurately, 'Being Is Being', which is Pure Being.

2. The Ancient One is a name of Kether, the first manifestation of the Ain Soph Aur, the three veils of 'negativity' that precede it. Kether is sometimes symbolised as the hilt of a flaming sword that proceeds from the mouth of God. In a sense, Kether is as the Malkuth of the Ain Soph Aur and is the first robe of the Ain, the Infinite. An image of Kether that consists of a bearded king seen in profile indicates that Kether has both a manifest and an unmanifest aspect.

3. The radiant light of Kether is called *mezla*—a word suggestive of stars or planets, for the celestial bodies have their seed source in the primordial swirling motion of the limitless 'sea of space' that is Kether—though we should remember these are analogous terms, and that Kether is not within space and time in reality. As the mundane chakra of Chokmah is Mazloth, the Zodiac, Kether corresponds to the fixed stars, more particularly the Pole star. The *mezla* is the 'dew' or transmission of a spiritual influence, likened in various traditions to fire, rain and lightning as well as the Sun—these four being the 'heavenly lights' mentioned in the *Upanishads* (Taittariya I.iii.2).

4. The magical power of Kether is Union with God, which is more akin to the yogic state of Samadhi than anything concerned with magick as such.

---

[17] Transliterated: ShKL MVPLA (numerical value 507).

The Illuminating or Radiant Intelligence

1. Chokmah, the second path, is called the Illuminating or Radiant Intelligence.[18] It is called the Crown of Creation and the Splendour of Unity: 'It is the Crown of Creation and the splendour of the Supreme Unity, to which it is most near in proximity. It is exalted above every head, and is distinguished as the Second Splendour'. Chokmah is the first full expression of duality, the dyad, and as such is also called the Second Glory. The type of unity referred to Chokmah, as the direct reflection of Kether, is that of the totality of all the possibilities of manifestation or being.

2. Chokmah is all-transcendent consciousness, the reflective pure-awareness of Kether, and so it is sometimes regarded as a feminine intelligence. Its meaning is identical to the Greek Sophia, Wisdom.[19] Understanding may be gained through the attitude (*mudra*) of the yogi whose concentration is directed inwards and upwards in *ajna*, the 'third-eye' chakra situated above the level of the physical eyes. This chakra is a mirror for the light of Kether (as *sahasrara*), a light that is itself a reflection of the Ain Soph Aur. Chokmah is also imaged as a bearded king or male figure. There is a 'phallic' aspect to the second path; geometrically it is the extension of the 'point' into the line or vertical polar axis. Chokmah is thus sometimes associated with ancient stone constructions, for example monolithic or circular groups of standing stones. The mundane chakra of Chokmah is Mazloth, the Zodiac, and this also leads to associations with the round table of King Arthur in the Celtic mysteries.[20]

3. In stillness and silence one may realise the self as a mirror for the infinite Self (Sanskrit Atma).

4. The magical power of Chokmah is the Vision of God (face to face). This is not complete or perfect Samadhi, as there is still separation between subject and object, but anyone that truly attains this is quite far along the path.

---

[18] ShKL MZHVR (608).

[19] Σοφια (781).

[20] For the detailed descriptions of the sephiroth in the four worlds of the Qabalah, which include divine, Archangelic, Angelic and chakra names, see *Hermetic Qabalah Foundation—Complete Course*.

The Sanctifying Intelligence

1. Binah, the third path, is called the Sanctifying Intelligence, and is also called the Foundation for the Primordial Wisdom (which is Chokmah).[21] It is also called the Mother of Faith—which in this sense is the power aspect of Ishwara or God called Shakti in Sanskrit, which has a direct equivalent with the Shekinah or feminine 'holy presence'. The Shakti, in all traditions, is the abode or dwelling of eternity, and the throne or seat of Knowledge.

2. As such, the Sanctifying Intelligence is inviolable, for it is the veritable Soul of God—it in no way arises from, or is conditioned by, the human ego or individual creature self.

3. Divine intuition is another term for the third path, for as faith or guidance it is beyond human comprehension, yet is the very soul and nature of all Intelligence and Understanding. The word 'intuition' used here has nothing to do with the 'instinctive' or 'subconscious'. Binah may be described as the field of Cosmic Intelligence, and as such it is sometimes considered to be the feminine aspect of Kether, in the same way that in Hinduism the Shakti is the feminine aspect of Brahma, Vishnu or Shiva. She then has a certain relation with Maya in the higher or cosmic sense. As the root of form, Binah is the type of all vehicles, all forms, yet her nature is formless. The cup is a symbol of Binah, as is the dove or higher intelligence; also the *yoni*.

4. The virtue of Binah is Silence, which is necessary for meditation and without which there can be no understanding of anything. The vice of Binah is Avarice, which is an inversion of the Shakti power of the production of forms from her own essence. The magical powers of Binah are the Vision of Sorrow and the Trance of Wonder. Sorrow and wonderment imply separation between subject and object but these may be viewed as a complementary pair, in which case they are unified and transcended in their higher principle, the Self (or Atma). Wonderment is *mufla* in Hebrew and is associated with Kether, the Primordial Light.[22] Sorrow is associated with tear drops and these are sometimes used in the same sense as celestial 'dew' or *mezla* (see Chokmah, the second path and the Vision of God).

---

[21] ShKL H-QDVSh (765).

[22] MVPLA (157)—the word is sometimes combined with 'intelligence', ShKL (350). *Mufla* has the meaning of 'hiding' or 'covering', which can refer to the sky or heaven as veiling the principle. Direct knowledge of the principle is incommunicable. 'Wonderment' conveys that which is *transmundane*.

The Measuring or Arresting Intelligence

1. Chesed or Gedulah, the fourth path, is the Measuring, Arresting or Receptacular Intelligence.[23] According to the *Book of Formation* this is so because 'it contains all the holy powers, and from it emanate all spiritual virtues with the most exalted essences; they emanate one from the other by the power of the primordial emanation' (Westcott). Kether is the Primordial Emanation and the 'exalted essences' are the life that pours forth into the 'cups' or receptacles of the Tree of Life. Chesed is thus sometimes compared to a fountain of living water. The word 'arresting' could also be translated 'capturing', for Chesed captures the descending influence or *mezla* (see the second path) and limits or contains it, while at the same time acting as support. It is said that 'Heaven covers while the Earth supports'. This is further reinforced by the symbolism of mountains that is associated with this sphere, and mountains, as well as being a link between heaven and earth, are also the source of rain and fire or lightning, which are further correspondences of *mezla* as spiritual influence. The number four of Chesed or Jupiter is always 'earth' in relation to the circle, which is 'heaven'. The square extends into the cube, and the six faces of the cube can symbolise the extremities of the three-dimensional cross with the six directions of space: above, below, north, south, east and west. It is the 'measure' of space.

2. At this level, manifest creatures, beings or angels cannot really be separate as such, so they are described as 'subtle emanations', and their difference is as a reverberation or reciprocal current, 'one from another'. As intelligences, they are not in any way individualities. Chesed is said to be the sphere of Cosmic Memory. This is sometimes misconstrued as the retention of the thoughts, words and deeds of individuals.

3. Chesed is sometimes referred to as the Sphere of the Masters. Presumably, this has some relation with the *bodhisattvas* in other traditions. It might also have come about through a relation between this fourth path, associated with *tzedek* or spiritual authority, and Melchizedek, the mysterious 'Prince of Peace' that appears in the book of Genesis 14: 18 to deliver a Eucharist of bread and wine:

> And Melchizedek king of Salem brought forth bread and wine: and he was the priest of the most high God.

Melchizedek is mentioned again in Psalms 110: 4:

> Thou art a priest for ever after the order of Melchizedek.

---

[23] ShKL QBVO (528).

4. The virtue of Chesed is Obedience (to the path). The vices of Chesed are Bigotry, Hypocrisy, Gluttony and Tyranny. At this level, the inverse aspects become magnified—one should always remember these are purely human traits that owe to a state of ignorance. The magical power attributed to Chesed is the Vision of Love, which is concerned with the beneficial nature of God or Shakti, and also to a certain extent the nature of a guru or an avatar, and of the disciples so blessed to follow the path.

The Radical Intelligence

1. Geburah, the fifth path, is called the Radical Intelligence.[24] It is so-called because 'it is more akin than any other to the Supreme Unity and emanates from the depths of the Primordial Wisdom'. The Primordial Wisdom is Chokmah, and one should bear in mind that the path receives this influence from the depths of Binah.

2. This confirms the relation of Geburah with the domain of the Shakti, or Hebrew Shekinah, the feminine Holy Spirit or 'divine presence'. Geburah is associated with all forms of justice and severity because its action is on the form side of the Tree. It therefore enforces the immutable laws and principles that are retained in the cosmic memory of Chesed. In Egyptian as well as Hindu tradition, the Shakti frequently manifests Justice and Peace, its complement.

3. One should remember that Geburah is negative to Binah and Chesed, but positive to Tiphereth and Hod. Geburah is the basis of the sense of an individual will, though that sense is an illusion arising from the ego's false idea of self as separate from Atma, the True Self, unconditioned.

4. The virtue of Geburah is Energy and Courage, which links the path with action or *karma*, and by which it has a special relation with Malkuth. The vice of Geburah is Cruelty and Destruction, which is misplaced energy and is at the same time also indicative of madness arising from the attachment to objects of desire. The magical power of Geburah is the Vision of Power, which in the proper sense is an attribute of the Shakti, who is the power aspect of God or Ishwara.

---

[24] Radical Intelligence: ShKL NShRSh (1,200).

The Mediating or Separative Intelligence

1. Tiphereth, the sixth path, is called the Mediating or Separative Intelligence.[25] It is called thus because 'it causes that influence to flow into all the reservoirs of the blessings with which these themselves are united' (Westcott). It is also said that 'the flux of the emanations is multiplied therein' (Waite). Tiphereth is at the centre of the middle pillar and the whole Tree of Life and, as such, is the heart of the universe and the true centre of man. As the centre, it is the place of the Mediator, which has its reflection in the priest or seer. Anything that is placed at the middle of two polar extremities also divides or separates that which is above from that which is below. Thus the sword is sometimes attributed to Christ.

2. Direct knowledge of this sphere is to partake of a certain degree of 'luminosity'; a symbol is no longer confused with that which it represents, for example.

3. In Tiphereth, all objects, creatures and things are named by the power of the Word. The separation referred to in the title is the discrimination by which everything is ordered according to its type and class. A *rite*, for example, means 'to set in order'. The three paths that connect Tiphereth with the lower triad of Netzach, Hod and Yesod are the routes by which human desire and intellect receive the influences of the sephiroth of the upper worlds. All personal action is derived from the cosmic source of life and activity that flows out of Tiphereth in the same way that the sun gives light and life to the world. If the sun went out or was not there, all life and activity would cease.

4. Tiphereth has a correspondence with the Sanskrit *jivatma*, the centre of the ego self or *ahankara*, which is a reflection of the Atma or True Self, in the same way that the sun may be reflected in a pool of water. The virtue of Tiphereth is therefore Devotion to the Great Work. The vice of the sephira, Pride, is the error of attributing all power to the personal ego. The magical power of Tiphereth is the Vision of the Harmony of Things.

---

[25] ShKL ShPO NBDL (886).

The Occult or Hidden Intelligence

1. Netzach, the seventh path, is called the Occult Intelligence, or the Hidden Intelligence.[26] It is called thus because 'it pours out a brilliant splendour on all intellectual virtues which are beheld with the eyes of spirit and by the ecstasy of faith'. In Netzach is the realisation that visible nature is the expression of the infinite or divine absolute. Netzach is the source of energy, desire and imagination and so is the sphere of the artist, the poet and the dreamer. The 'eyes of spirit' means here unclouded perception or understanding. Understanding and faith are both attributes of Binah, the third path, indicating there is a special relation with Netzach. Saturn, it may be noted, is the seventh chakra counting upward from the Moon in the natural order of the sephiroth. Binah is the house of the Shekinah or Holy Spirit, and through Saturn (Shabbathai) is associated with rest and peace. On the lower arc, the sphere of Venus may see an excitation of dreams and imagining, to the extent that one can be driven be restless agitation, through attachment to the objects of desire.

2. Netzach is at the base of the pillar of force, and so the practitioner on this path is very susceptible to being deceived by illusionary splendours. The Occult Intelligence is the intelligence of hiding or veiling; all of visible nature is a symbol for metaphysical reality. The senses are therefore the veil that conceals the power of the seventh path. Penetrating the mysteries of the seventh path and overcoming the potential for delusion requires right action (*karma*), which involves necessary sacrifices and austerities. It requires faith, which is a divine gift and must also be recognised as such.

3. The aspirant must therefore gain control of faculties that usually control, dominate and enslave the unawakened human being.

4. The virtue of Netzach is Unselfishness. 'Wrong actions' (*karma*) are the fruits of selfishness. The vice of Netzach is Unchastity, which is not being faithful to the chosen path. One may learn much from gods or deities, but without faith in the guru or teacher, which also means that action is taken on the advice received, such knowledge cannot be made effective. The magical power attributed to the sphere of Netzach is the Vision of Beauty Triumphant.

---

[26] ShKL NSThR (1,060).

The Perfect Intelligence

1. Hod, the eighth path, is called the Perfect Intelligence.[27] It is so-called because 'it is the dwelling place of the Primordial, and has no root in which it may abide other than the recesses of Gedulah whence its essence emanates.' Hod is at the base of the pillar of form. It is negative to Geburah and Tiphereth but positive to Yesod and Malkuth.

2. The title from the *Book of Formation* gives the hint that Hod derives its essence from Chesed or Gedulah, two planes above and on the opposite side of the Tree. What we experience in ordinary life seems to be a chain of causality arising from our own actions, so that our decisions and choices between this thing and that thing seem really important. Yet this feeling arises from the resistance to the flow of cosmic force that creates the illusion of separate mind, body and will on the plane of action. Paradoxically, we do have the power to arrange things and order them 'at will'. When we arrange and order things in accordance with the timeless wisdom or authentic teaching, then we become participants in the Great Work. It is said in the *Upanishads* that the union of the teacher and the disciple is through the mantras (Taittariya I.iii.3)—that is to say, the correct sounding of the prayers and invocations central to the rites.

3. Hod is also called the Stellar Light, which is a key to the magical vision of the sphere. The illusion of power at this level is very great, for it is where the falsely illuminated see the finger pointing at the Moon: they see the body of teaching or the guru or teacher himself, but whether there is good faith in that or not, they do not perceive the truth that is indicated. In that way, Hod is the sphere of all religions and religious teachings, yet is also the sphere of science. Science and religion often unite in times of war, at other times they are at war with each other. In fact, they are as much alike as twins in a single pod, for neither can perceive truth directly.

4. The virtue of Hod is Truthfulness, and this is associated with right speech and also, as mentioned above, the verity of the sacred rites. The vice of Hod is Falsehood and Dishonesty. The magical power attributed to Hod is the Vision of Splendour, which amounts to a vision of the operations of the angels of God, which are no less than the attributes of deity in active mode.

---

[27] ShKL ShLM (720).

The Pure Intelligence

1. Yesod, the ninth path, is called the Pure Intelligence.[28] It is called thus because 'it purifies the sephiroth, proves and preserves their images, and prevents them from destruction or division by their union with itself'. This may be better put, 'it is the purifying essence of the sephiroth', for the Hebrew title means 'pure or complete'. It is the supreme principle undetermined, as reflected downwards upon the Foundation. It is through the union or knowledge of the supreme principle that all dross, or all conditioning, is removed. Yesod is negative to all the sephiroth except Malkuth, to which it is positive. Here, the side of force and the side of form meet in powerful union. The magical image of Yesod is reputed to be that of a man with an erect phallus, for Yesod is the sphere of the generative organs in both male and female. A naked feminine deity such as that of Ishtar could equally apply. Manifested forms are produced from their principle—the 'excitement' involved has nothing to do with sexual arousal as such. The source of manifestation is unmanifest in itself.

2. The dual nature of the Moon gives a clue to the surging of the tides and fluxes through the astral plane, which has its equivalent in the subtle modalities of the individuality. The ninth path is sometimes called the Treasure House of Images, for it is a repository for all images and their types as impressed upon the aethyr or *akasha*—for this reason the Akashic Records are said to be stored here, on the cosmic level.

3. The 'distillation of essence' implied by the ninth path is portrayed in the Angel's cauldron in Tarot Atu XIV, Temperance.

4. The virtue of Yesod is Independence. There is an inversion of this, where independence is sought vainly and almost unconsciously by refusing to follow the teaching, especially if that requires some effort. The vice of Yesod is therefore Idleness. The power of self-deception can be such that the idle man will not think he is idle, because there is still activity—but the activity is going everywhere else but to that one thing chosen. Such activity can be either physical or mental. The idleness then becomes more a matter of weakness of will or simple foolishness—the 'stubborn ass' (see p. 60). The magical power of the path is the Vision of the Secret Nature of the Universe.[29]

---

[28] ShKL THVR (570).

[29] This is quite often called the 'Machinery of the Universe' (Crowley's *777* for example), which owes to a Cartesian mechanistic view of Nature.

The Resplendent Intelligence

1. Malkuth, the tenth path, is called the Resplendent Intelligence.[30] It is called thus because 'it is exalted above every head and has its seat in Binah; it illuminates the splendour of all the lights and causes the flowing forth of influence from the Prince of Countenances'. The title of the tenth path is a reminder that Malkuth is Kether, but after another fashion. Malkuth is sometimes confused with the planet earth, but is the sum and resultant of all manifestation. The Prince of Countenances is a title of Kether, and there is also a relation with Metatron and the Shekinah. In this context, the Shekinah or the feminine Holy Spirit is understood to be hidden in Malkuth, in much the same way that in the Hindu Tantras, Kundalini Shakti is coiled and dreaming there. It is through the descending influx from the Prince of Countenances that she awakens and climbs towards him, so to speak. She is also said to cause this influence by her presence, for the two are only separate from the point of view of man in the fallen state.

2. The Qliphoth or world of Shells is said to be beneath Malkuth, for the roots of a tree plunge as deeply into the earth as the branches reach to the heavens. Malkuth has a particular resonance with Geburah for it is known as a sphere of action or *karma*. Malkuth is sometimes called the Bride, Malkah, for she awaits the coming of her Lord (Adonai). That is to say, she is the faithful soul that will be awakened by spirit. Hence the vision of the Holy Guardian Angel is ascribed to this sephira. Discrimination is the first virtue of the path, the Way, yet the worldly person exercises this power in ignorance, imagining that nothing exists above or beyond the realm of the human individuality. Thus the worldly revere ignorance, believing it to be truth, and hate wisdom, closing their eyes and ears to it—for wisdom contradicts all that they wish to hold to so as to maintain a false notion of self.

3. The Holy Living Creatures of Kether become the Kerubim, the angels of the four elements in Malkuth. The Kerub of Malkuth is the Sphinx, which is a composite of the four Holy Living Creatures. The secret of Malkuth is that the Kingdom of Heaven is always present in reality, and so it does not truly come about in a future age or time, neither will it come about through physical death, though it appears that way from the perspective of fallen man, bound by time. Malkuth is *in reality* the Temple of the Eternal, and there is nothing that can done either to bring this about or to prevent it, for it is a spiritual and literal fact—one can only recognise it or not.

---

[30] ShKL MThNVTzTz (1,836).

4. The virtue of Malkuth is Discrimination, and this is therefore said to be the first virtue on the path. The vice of Malkuth is Inertia and Avarice, for refusal to take the right action on the plane of action leads to an inversion of the principle that is forever present. Avarice is thus the attempt to store up treasures that are no more than phenomenal illusions. In various traditions, there is said to be a dragon that guards the real treasure stored up at the foot of the Tree of Life. The magical power attributed to Malkuth is the Vision of the Holy Guardian Angel, or Adonai, which is no less than the vision of God.

א

The Scintillating or Fiery Intelligence

1. Aleph, the eleventh path, connects Kether the Crown with Chokmah, the sphere of the Zodiac. The path is called the Scintillating Intelligence.[31] The Yetziratic text says that the path is the 'veil placed before the dispositions and order of superior and inferior causes. Whosoever possesses this path is in the enjoyment of great dignity; to possess it is to be face to face with the Cause of Causes'. The path is in the nature of a veil since it is the first path of transmission for the Ain Soph Aur or Limitless Light through Kether. The superior cause is Kether, Pure Being. Chokmah, the inferior cause, is highly exalted but is nonetheless secondary to the first cause. The veil is the reflection, which must be transcended before supreme reality can be known.

2. The position of the eleventh path, above the Abyss, denotes that it is quite far beyond the level of the ordinary human intellect or reason. On descent of the path, the formless spirit is clothed in manifestation by degrees. Thus the infinite is concealed in the finite, in names and numbers, principles and principalities. Ascending the path in the fullest sense is the vision of being face to face with God, which has its equivalent in higher degrees of yoga Samadhi, though not the highest.

3. The inverse aspect of the inexpressible vision of the Seer is irrationality and madness in all its forms. This has a dual aspect: a real seer or truly enlightened sage may be seen as a madman by the profane, and in rare cases he may even choose for it to be that way, as a kind of cover or protection. This has nothing to do with ordinary madness, which owes to loss of all contact with a higher principle.

---

[31] ShKL MTzVChTzCh (592).

4. The eleventh path is imaged forth by the Tarot key the Fool 0, which is also called the Spirit of Aethyr. The magical power of the path is said to be that of Divination, which probably owes to a particular idea of the Order of the Golden Dawn where the Great Angel HRU is set over the operation of the Tarot as the power of the lightning flash, which has the hilt in Kether and commences along the eleventh path. Aleph has a correspondence with the element of air, as does the Qabalistic world of Yetzirah.

ב

The Intelligence of Light or Transparency

1. Beth, the twelfth path, connects Kether the Crown with Binah, the sphere of Saturn. The path is called the Intelligence of Light.[32] It is called thus 'because it is the image of magnificence. It is said to be the source of vision in those who behold visions'. According to Westcott, the word *bhir* translates as 'transparency'. Either way, this refers to the fluidic mercurial light or essence (ATh or Azoth) for which this path is a medium or channel. The intelligence of the path is the divine power of producing vessels for light at the cosmic level. As the nature of the light is formless, it requires the enclosure or dwelling inherent in the letter *beth* to produce differentiated beings, though these are not in any way to be considered as individualities at this level.

2. The letter *beth* means 'a house', or more precisely, a nomad's tent that is open at the front. At this level the dwelling place is that which encloses the principle itself, rendering it intelligible to the lower worlds of being. It is therefore a medium for the transmission of the Primordial Light into the field of the cosmic matrix in Binah.

3. The Yetziratic text says that the twelfth path is 'the source of vision in those who behold visions'. The mercurial light can then be taken as more or less equal to the Sanskrit *prana*, 'breath' or 'spirit', which has its lower analogue in the five senses, both subtle and physical. The power of true vision is seeing into the nature of things, which requires discrimination. Yet it is by the same power that phantoms or apparitions are perceived, that is, the unreal. To see these for what they truly are is a further aspect of true vision.

---

[32] ShKL BHIR (567).

4. The twelfth path is imaged forth by the Tarot key the Magician I, which also has the title the Magus of Power. The Golden Dawn correspondence of the letter *beth* is Mercury, which differs from that given in the *Book of Formation*—though different codices vary:

> He caused the letter ‏ב‎ to reign in Wisdom, bound a crown upon it and fused them together. He produced by means of them: the Sun in the Universe, Sunday in the year, and the right eye in Man, male and female.

The magical powers of the twelfth path are the Miracles of Healing, the Gift of Tongues and the Knowledge of Sciences, which are all correspondences of Mercury. The 'miracles of healing' are a kind of 'accidental' product of yogis or avatars that have reached a certain level. None of these have ever placed any great importance in such magical powers. The 'gift of tongues' is not to be taken too literally, though there have been many deluded persons that have sought to produce such an effect by babbling nonsense, which is a kind of parody of the real power. It should be remembered that the tongue is not only concerned with speech but also hearing, to which it is closely allied. This has nothing to do with languages in the sense of physical utterance. The 'knowledge of sciences' of course refers to traditional sciences, which are never understood separately from a whole body of teaching or doctrine.

‏ג‎

The Uniting Intelligence

1. Gimel, the thirteenth path, connects Kether the Crown with Tiphereth, the sphere of the Sun. The thirteenth path is called the Uniting Intelligence.[33] It is called thus because it is 'the perfection of the truths of spiritual unities'. It is the medium by which the light, spiritual influence or *mezla* from Kether is conveyed to Tiphereth, which also reflects all of the paths of the Tree.

2. The number of the thirteenth path is equal to 'unity' (*achad*). Tiphereth, the sixth path, is the centre of the individuality, the near equivalent to the Sanskrit *jiva*, which reflects the Atma or True Self as the image of the sun is reflected in a pool or water. The Atma is impressed by the *boddhi* or higher intellectual intuition, which is likened to a ray from the sun. A further comparison might then be made with Da'ath, Knowledge, which is usually figured as a phantom circle on the thirteenth path between Kether and Tiphereth.

---

[33] ShKL MNHIG HA-ChDVTh (882).

Da'ath has a dual aspect: as mediator between the primordial source and the centre of the egoistic self-awareness, it may be likened to the Sanskrit *boddhi*; much has been made of the Abyss, which is the inferior aspect of Da'ath as an inverse reflection. This can be figured by a tetrahedronal pyramid with the first three sephiroth as the base and Da'ath as the apex—the pyramid is inverse, however, and some comparison may be drawn with the Hanged Man of Tarot, who is suspended upside down from the world tree.

3. It is interesting that unity seems to appear here in the text in the plural form, yet there can be said to be a kind of multiplicity inherent in unity when that is considered as a secondary principle to that which is supreme (Atma). We may assume that 'unities' refers to that, and not to any sort of atomism, unless that somehow found its way into the esotericism of the Hebrews. The title is sometimes construed as 'unitive' but that would refer more to the fact that all separative determinations are unified in the supreme principle.

4. The thirteenth path is imaged forth by Tarot Atu the Priestess II. The trump is also known as Priestess of the Silver Star. The magical powers of the path are that of the White Tincture, Clairvoyance and of Divination by Dreams. These powers really refer to the subtle aspects afforded the Moon, as a summation of the non-corporeal states that are nonetheless still in the domain of form. The higher aspects of the path reach to the formless states of being.

ד

The Luminous Intelligence

1. The fourteenth path of Daleth connects Chokmah, the sphere of the Zodiac, with Binah, the sphere of Saturn. The path is called the Luminous or Illuminating Intelligence.[34] 'It is the institutor of arcana, the foundation of holiness.' This is because the path proceeds from Chokmah, the source of light or intelligence, to Binah, which is the 'throne' or foundation of intelligence at the supernal level.

2. The foundation of holiness is the dwelling or abode of the Shekinah, Binah. The fourteenth path is the transmission of light-intelligence along the first horizontal bar of the lightning flash. The letter *daleth* means 'a door', or 'doorbolt'. At this level, the gate is the source of all manifestation as well as the means of passing out of manifestation to return to the supreme principle forever.

---

[34] ShKL MAIR (601).

3. The fourteenth path is the conjunction or union between Will and Understanding at the cosmic level. The conjunction of divine names sometimes used for Da'ath as the 'resultant' of the two is therefore Tetragrammaton Elohim or IAO Elohim. In terms of the microcosm, Da'ath is then an outward aspect of the *ajna* chakra—the Sanskrit *ajna* also means 'knowledge'. Chokmah and Binah are then identical with the two petals of the lotus placed here in the Tantras. The intensely creative, generative power of the path when viewed from the corporeal point of view owes to its root in Chokmah, the seed of light at the primary level, and its termination in Binah, the womb of all nascent life.

4. The fourteenth path is imaged forth by Tarot Atu the Empress III. The trump is also called the Daughter of the Mighty Ones. The magical power of the path is that of Love-philtres, a correspondence of Venus.

ה

The Constituting Intelligence

1. The fifteenth path of Hé connects Chokmah, the sphere of the Zodiac, with Tiphereth, the sphere of the Sun. The path is called the Constituting Intelligence.[35] It is called thus 'because it constitutes the substance of creations in pure darkness' (Westcott). Waite added that it is the same darkness mentioned in the book of Job 38: 9, 'the cloud and the envelope thereof'.

2. This cloud of 'thick darkness' mentioned in the book of Job is the covering of the sea, or the firmament, and is that which contains or holds it. It is therefore fitting that the Egyptian goddess of the night sky, Nuit, should be referred to the fifteenth path. There is also a certain correspondence with the Sanskrit *prakriti* or 'substance', from which the five envelopes or sheaths of being are produced. Each envelope is a covering or hiding of Atma, the Real.

The five also relate to the 'star' of Nuit, which has five rays and forms the *jivatma* or creature soul, Tiphereth as the centre of the ego. As such, this is at a level of darkness or ignorance as seen from the point of view of the supreme absolute.

---

[35] ShKL MOMID (514).

3. Chokmah is the chakra of the Zodiac, as separate and distinct from the fixed stars, which are the domain of Kether and the North Pole of the universe. The Zodiac is the belt or girdle of Venus, the planetary symbol of Nuit in her manifestation as visible nature. Tiphereth, at the further end of this path, is the recipient for the spiritual influence or starry *mezla* that is transmitted from Chokmah.

4. The fifteenth path is imaged forth by the Tarot trump the Star XVII. The trump is also called Daughter of the Firmament: Dweller between the Waters. Owing to that which has already been pointed out above, it is necessary to counterchange the Tarot trumps on the fifteenth and twenty-eighth paths, for Aries, previously assigned to the fifteenth path, is the sign of the fire of blood, the blood of the Lamb as depicted in Christian symbolism. Aquarius, on the other hand, is the Waters of Space, typified by the Egyptian hieroglyph of two streams of water or radiation, and really symbolises heaven, or states of being that are beyond form altogether. The magical power of the fifteenth path is that of Astrology, as Aquarius is the sign of the heavens. This should not be confused with popular notions of astrology.

ו

The Triumphant or Eternal Intelligence

1. The sixteenth path of Vav connects Sophia or Chokmah, the sphere of the Zodiac, with Chesed the magnificent or glorious sphere of Jupiter. The path is called the Triumphant or Eternal Intelligence.[36] It is called 'the delight of glory, the paradise of pleasure prepared for the just'. It is therefore the way of return to the Garden of Eden. The paradise referred to is the 'salvation' of the soul by its prolongation in other states of being; this does not refer to the Sanskrit *moksha* 'liberation', or final deliverance, which means leaving manifestation forever, although the soul thus saved still has a chance of this at the end of time, or the end of a Cosmic Cycle.

2. The descent of the path is aptly figured in the letter *vav*, where the creative seed or the essential fire is driven downwards towards manifestation. Looked at another way, the *vav* is the head and stem of the phallus (or spinal column), which, in the cosmic sense, is the pillar of the light or primordial consciousness of *aur* or *prana*, which is placed symbolically upon the world axis. The name of the letter *vav* means 'a nail' or 'pin', which is a further symbol of the polar axis, in this case reaching downward through all worlds.

---

[36] ShKL NTzChI (508).

3. The power of imagining is an attribute of Venus, the planetary ruler of Taurus and the earthly form of Nuit, as depicted on the previous fifteenth path. The Moon is exalted in Taurus; the lunar nature of this path is that it reflects the dark radiance or essence that pours forth from the Ain Soph into Chesed, the sphere of Jupiter.

4. The sixteenth path is imaged by the Pope or Hierophant V, which is also called the Magus of the Eternal. To hear the 'voice' or subtle vibration of the Hierophant is to receive initiatic transmission and to commence the glorious return implicit in the path's title from the *Book of Formation*. As the Way-shower, the inner teacher or higher intuition, the Magus of the Eternal reminds us that if we follow the word-vibration back to its source in the infinite, all phenomena cease to exist.

The magical power of the sixteenth path is the Secret of Physical Strength. The secret bears no relation to athleticism, for it is the knowledge of that which animates all things that live and move and have their being. The Word or Logos conveys secret knowledge of the True Will (Atma although, in a more limited sense, Dharma).

ז

The Intelligence of Sensation

1. The seventeenth path of Zain connects Binah, the sphere of Saturn, with Tiphereth, the sphere of the Sun. The path is called the Intelligence of Sensation or the Disposing Intelligence.[37] 'It disposes the devout to perseverance, and thus prepares them to receive the Holy Spirit'. It is also called the Foundation of Tiphereth in the plane of the Supernals—for its root is in Binah and its termination is in the centre of the Ruach.

2. The word for 'sensation' in the title derives from the root meaning of agitation, stirring or seething (*ha-regash*)—the reason is much troubled by the dualism inherent in its own nature, yet it is this turbulent state of affairs that is necessary before any Great Work can begin. The agitation is calmed down when the illusionary nature of all phenomena is understood. The five senses are the support for all mental perceptions, which produce what the ignorant man mistakes for reality.

---

[37] ShKL H-HRGSh (863).

3. Path seventeen is the seventh from Aleph. Its letter *zain* (or *zayin*) is the sword separating the waters of the Firmament of Nu into the twin streams of time and space. It is thus the power of the Word or Logos, reflected downward upon the lower worlds of manifestation.

4. The seventeenth path is imaged forth by Tarot Atu the Lovers VI, which is also called the Children of the Voice: Oracle of the Mighty Gods. The duality of the seventeenth path is expressed in alchemical pairs such as Sol and Luna, or Mars and Venus. This is depicted in the imagery of the Tarot trump as a wedding presided over (or secretly observed) by Hermes or Mercury. The magical powers of the path are the Power of being in two or more places at once, and of Prophecy. This owes obviously to the dual nature of Gemini and its ruling planet Mercury.

ח

The Intelligence of the House of Influence

1. The eighteenth path of Cheth connects Binah, the sphere of Saturn, with that of Geburah, the sphere of Mars. The path is called the Intelligence of the House of Influence.[38] It is called thus because from 'thence are drawn the arcana and the concealed meanings that repose in the shadow thereof'. It is also said of this path that by the greatness of its abundance, 'the influx of good things upon created beings is increased'. Cheth means 'a wall' or 'enclosure'. The power or intelligence of the eighteenth path is experienced as a sea of light or joy that flows like water from the primordial fount. It then has a relationship with the higher degrees of Savikalpa Samadhi, as well as the lower ones, in which knowledge of any object of meditation (*dhyana*) is gained.

2. Much of the labour of the Great Work is to make the frail human personality a suitable vehicle for the influx of cosmic consciousness that would otherwise overwhelm it. The preliminary work is always to train the mind and to increase the power of concentration—one must hold an image steady in the mind, like an unwavering flame.

---

[38] ShKL BITh H-ShPO (1,217).

3. The Holy Ghost and the Holy Graal are cognate terms, for the Cup of Binah is the receptacle from which the feminine spirit, the holy Shekinah, is imbibed as sacred *soma*, or total knowledge, resulting in divine intoxication. Such 'intoxication' is frequently confused with ordinary drunkenness or the use of mind-changing drugs but divinity cannot in any way be produced from the human mind or body.

4. The eighteenth path is imaged forth by Tarot Atu the Chariot VII, which is also called the Child of the Powers of the Waters: Lord of the Triumph of Light. The mental powers, once concentration is learned, may be applied to the building of a Chariot or Merkebah. The Chariot is a vehicle by which the subtle paths of the Hermetic Tree may be negotiated.

The magical power of Cheth the eighteenth path is that of Casting Enchantments. One should be wary then of misunderstanding these runes; the subtle plane is no more than a field of modalities of the individual state that represent a prolongation of that state. Magical transformation and the power of spells in general might be added here, as the Egyptian scarab Khephra is the equivalent of the zodiacal sign of Cancer the Crab.

ט

The Intelligence of the Secret of Spiritual Activities

1. The nineteenth path of Teth connects Chesed, the sphere of Jupiter, with Geburah, the sphere of Mars. The path is called the Intelligence of the Secret of all Spiritual Activities.[39] It is thus called because 'the fullness which it receives is derived from the highest benediction and the supreme glory'. It is also called the path of Peace and Misfortune, which is better understood as Peace and Justice, for these are dual aspects of the Shekinah or Holy Spirit, to which this path relates.

2. The nineteenth path is the first that is wholly beneath the Abyss when descending, and the last before the Abyss when ascending the Tree; it is therefore the secret ruler and governor of all that is below, even as it receives the influence (*mezla*) from that which is above. The 'benediction' most likely refers to the sphere of Chesed, which has an association with Melchizedek the Prince of Peace, through Tzedek, the name of the mundane chakra of Jupiter, all of which conveys a sense of priestly blessing. Also, Chesed or Gedulah receives its influence from the supernal sephiroth—in the *Book of Formation*, everything is related to its higher principle.

---

[39] ShKL SVD H-POVLVTh H-RVChNIVTh (1,702).

3. The secret of the path, as such, is that material nature veils or conceals the numinous source of all. Another way of looking at this is that all of nature is a symbol, exactly as according to the Vedanta, the Sun or the rayed face of a Lion may symbolise God or Ishwara, which in turn is realised as Brahma. Thus the Sun is called the Gate of Brahma, which to the Egyptians was Ra.

4. The nineteenth path is imaged forth by the Tarot trump Force or Strength XI, which is also called the Daughter of the Flaming Sword. The earlier versions of the Tarot trump, such as the first printed Tarot of Marseilles, depict a curious form of what the ancient Egyptians termed as the 'Opening of the Mouth'. The woman appears to be either opening or closing the mouth of a lion or other beast, which links the path with oracular powers. As the path is placed immediately below Da'ath, there is a ready correspondence with the *vishuddha* chakra that is in turn associated with the sense of hearing and of sound vibration. Compared to the Egyptian ritual of 'opening the mouth', the trump may also allude to the soul's continued life after death, through power of utterance of the magical spells as well as the fourth power of the Sphinx, to Keep Silence. The magical power of the path is said to be the Power of Training Wild Beasts, which may be better construed as the *knowledge of the language of birds and animals*—both of which may be a symbol for angels or celestial (i.e., supra-human) intelligences.

The Intelligence of Will

1. The twentieth path of Yod connects Chesed, the sphere of Jupiter, with Tiphereth, the sphere of the Sun. The path is the Intelligence of Will.[40] It is called thus 'because it prepares all created beings, each individually, for the demonstration of the existence of the primordial glory'. The *Book of Formation* gives the letter of this path as *tav*, and its correspondence Saturn, whereas here it is *yod* and Virgo.

However, the letter *yod* is the primary basis of all the other letters, and its uppermost tip or 'point' symbolises the supreme principle. The perfection and purity of Virgo underlines this. The path may be compared with the ray of light or intelligence forming the innermost structures of the mental faculties in man, called *manas* in Sanskrit, the 'inward sense'. Ascending the twentieth path fully constitutes the realisation of the integrality of total being or Universal Man.

---

[40] ShKL H-RTzVN (701).

2. On this path arises the possibility of knowing the True Will or Self (Atma), through the ray of light or intelligence called the *boddhi* in Sanskrit.

3. The zodiacal sign of this path is Virgo, associated with Isis as the virgin mother. The descent of this path brings the ray of light from the higher intelligence to realisation in Tiphereth, the centre of the individual creature soul. The Pythagorean number of the path is 210, an indication of NOX or Night as the unmanifest at the formless level. The trinity of the number 210 is summed up in the staff, lamp and cloak of the Hermit; the 'cloak of invisibility' is the silent means of transmission of an initiatic current.

4. The twentieth path is imaged by Tarot Atu the Hermit IX, which is also called the Prophet of the Eternal: Magus of the Voice of Power. The seed of the letter *yod* of this path is sometimes symbolised as a *bindu* or 'wound' in a heart, which is the true centre of the being, so to speak, and which contains within its 'cave' or cavity the essence of all. The magical powers of the path are said to be those of Invisibility, Parthenogenesis and Initiation. The 'child' that is born in secrecy and silence, not by any generative means, is the Flower of Mind or Sanskrit *boddhi*, the higher intellect that is able to perceive the Atma or uppermost tip of the *yod* directly, without distortion through the mental faculties that cleave to sensorial objects. Initiation is a silent 'vibration' that is transmitted through a tradition or organisation, or its representatives.

כ

The Intelligence of Desirous Quest

1. The twenty-first path of Kaph connects Chesed, the sphere of Jupiter, with Netzach, the sphere of Venus. The twenty-first path is called the Intelligence of Desire, or the Rewarding Intelligence.[41] It is called thus because 'it receives the divine influence, and it influences by its benediction all existing things'.

The word for 'desire' used here is *meboqash*, and this also has the meaning of 'hunger', 'thirst' and 'emptiness'. The need for fulfilment, the seeking out of 'something' yearned for, is a false premise based on the emptiness or non-existence of the human ego as relative to the principle of the Self (or Atma). It is nonetheless necessary to even begin the quest for true Knowledge, in which case all desire is turned towards that end.

---

[41] ShKL ChPTz H-MBVQSh (631, 986).

2. Netzach is the lowest outpost of the pillar of force on the plane of desire, and is associated with the seductive glamour of the astral plane or subtle world. The magnifying power of Chesed added to the magnetism of Netzach creates intense longing.

3. The quest for something needed to make life complete is illusory unless the desire is turned inwards through the hard discipline of meditation indicated by the twenty-third path of the Hanged Man on the opposite side of the Tree. Chesed holds the key to true knowledge of the Self, yet the same deep well of influence also has the capacity to enthral those hungry for self-substantiation with glamorous and self-aggrandising fantasies of 'past lives' lived as a high priest, queen, princess, a victim or martyr, and so forth. In fact, all intense desires for self-substantiation, where there is a seeking of self-identity in all manner of shapes and forms, including quite perverse notions, is derived from the averse or demonic aspect of this path. The anger and hostility that often accompanies this, directed against all others that do not share in the particular delusion, is a sign of the demonic nature of the influence on the personality, which degrades it.

4. The twenty-first path is imaged by the Tarot trump Fortune or the Wheel X. It is the wheel of cyclical rebirth in the manifest worlds, which is often confused with erroneous 'reincarnation'. The magical power of the twenty-first path is that of Acquiring Political and other Ascendency. Political ascendancy, a correspondence of Jupiter, can be construed as political 'influence', which is an inversion of the true power of the path.

ל

The Faithful Intelligence

1. The twenty-second path of Lamed connects Geburah, the sphere of Mars, with Tiphereth, the sphere of the Sun. The twenty-second path is called the Faithful Intelligence.[42] It is said by this path 'spiritual virtues are deposited and augment therein, until they pass to those who dwell under the shadow thereof'. The spiritual powers are then increased, so to speak, or extended. Westcott gave this as 'all dwellers on earth are under its shadow'. This alludes to the Justice aspect on the Form side of the Tree, as opposed to Peace, its complement. The shadow is the inversion of the spiritual virtue or power seen from the point of view of ignorance, for deeds and actions will then lead to an increase of suffering.

---

[42] ShKL NAMN (491).

2. This path is reflected on the other side of the Tree by that of the Hermit—the cloaked Hermes-Mercury. The twentieth path conveys the knowledge of the True Will, reflected in the form of transmission or vibration from the Primordial Wisdom into the upwelling fountain of Chesed. The twenty-second path conveys the spiritual power to know that all thoughts, words and actions are the expression of the True Self, though made subject to determination and contingency through the ignorance implicit in the lower nature.

3. One must not then confuse the personal will, prone as it is to conditions and modifications, with the True Self or Will, which is the cause of all conditions without being in any way subject to those conditions.

4. The twenty-second path is imaged forth by Tarot trump Justice VIII, which is also called Daughter of the Lords of Truth: Ruler of the Balance. The magical powers of the twenty-second path are Works of Justice and Equilibrium, which are complementary. Both owe to the correspondence with Libra, and both are attributes of the Shakti or Shekinah, otherwise Shekinah and Metatron.

מ

The Stable Intelligence

1. The twenty-third path of Mem connects Geburah, the sphere of Mars, with Hod, the sphere of Mercury. The path is called the Stable Intelligence.[43] It is the 'source of consistency in all the numerations'. This refers to the permanence or stability of all the sephiroth. We are reminded that the letter *mem* of the path involves the *yod* or seed principle, extended towards the formation of a vessel, which denotes the prehensile nature of water.

2. This path requires that we extend, sustain and prolong the yoga meditation. In the language of alchemy, it is to 'fix the volatile'.

3. Technically speaking, the Initiate of this twenty-third path should have mastered the art of *dhyana* (true meditation) and now aspires to attain *samadhi* (complete union of subject and object).

---

[43] ShKL QIIM (510).

4. The path is imaged forth by the Tarot Atu the Hanged Man XII, and which is also called the Spirit of the Mighty Waters. The Initiate is shown fixed to the Tree of Life, in a reversed posture. This forms, in the old tarots, the symbol of alchemical Sulphur reversed, which is the completion of the Great Work. The magical powers of the path are the Great Work, Talismans and Crystal gazing. Talismans relate to the twenty-third path through the 'fixing of the volatile', if we understand that as forming a substantial basis for the influence of the spiritual Idea. Crystal gazing symbolises the clear sight of the master of *samadhi*; it should not be confused with mere divination, which is only a simple application of the law of correspondences.

ב

The Imaginative Intelligence

1. The twenty-fourth path of Nun connects Tiphereth, the sphere of the Sun, with Netzach, the sphere of Venus. The path is called the Intelligence of Resemblance or Imaginative Intelligence.[44] The path is called thus because 'it is the ground of similarity in the likeness of beings who are created to its agreement after its aspects'.

The root of the Hebrew word for 'resemblance' or 'imagination' (DMINVI) means 'of blood'. It may therefore refer to type, caste or species. On its descent, this path culminates in Netzach, the seventh sephira, in which appears a diversity of creatures and things, all according to their type, caste or mould, so to speak. None of these are ever exactly the same, or 'replicated', but they are governed by the same set of principles or determinations, by which they are what they are.

2. While the principles that govern diverse forms do not include replication, and so uniformity, the modern age has developed a tendency to artificially bring about such uniformity through the suppression of all true unity. Thus the ideals of the modern world, typically 'diversity' and 'equality', which seem on the face of it to be completely reasonable, only serve to suppress any true unified state and promote homogeneity in all things, until individuals become no more than units, each completely identical to all else, so that any differences remaining are only the differences of one unitive product from another.

---

44 ShKL DMIVNI (470).

3. The descent of this path passes from the centre of the creature self in Tiphereth towards the desire plane of Netzach in order to bring about multiple and diverse modes of expression, vehicles for the self. On the way of return, such vehicles are transcended.

4. The twenty-fourth path is imaged forth by the Tarot Atu Death XIII, which is also called Child of the Great Transformers: Lord of the Gate of Death. In the post-mortem state, the various vehicles of the self are withdrawn and return to the undifferentiated (Sanskrit *prakriti*). The magical power of the twenty-fourth path is that of Necromancy, which is often mistaken for a kind of communication with human 'spirits', whereas in fact what remains temporarily on the subtle plane after death is not human strictly speaking, as it lacks a corporeal modality.

ס

The Intelligence of Probation

1. The twenty-fifth path of Samekh connects Tiphereth, the sphere of the Sun, with Yesod, the sphere of the Moon. The title of the path is Intelligence of Temptation or Trial, sometimes given as Probation or Trial.[45] The path is called thus because 'it is the first temptation by which God tests the devout'. Here it is called 'first temptation' from the point of view of ascending the paths upwardly from Malkuth.

2. Something in the nature of a sacrifice has to be undergone so that the harmony and beauty of Tiphereth is permanently established (and so realised) in the natural soul or body. Aspirants often fail on this path without ever realising that the fault was due to their own predispositions. It is difficult for the modern person to understand any notion of sacrifice at all without distortion, and so that makes it very difficult for any sacrifice to be made in the first place! At this level we are really dealing with the mental and psychological ground of the aspirant. So long as this is thought to be a ground worthy of clinging to, it then remains a permanent obstruction to any further progress. For example, the magical circle is put there to seal off the operation of the work from all external forces that would serve to limit it or misdirect the invoked powers. A person cannot maintain any social, political or other affiliations, even in their thoughts, let alone believe such opinions to have any validity.

---

45 ShKL NISVNI (536).

3. The operation of the Great Work can only proceed if the aspirant refuses to identify their self with the actions of the personality and the events that seem to be taking place around. The indifference is not to be thought of as any lack of attention; the level of observation is intensified through the meditation practice. All activity supposed to be 'personal' is then realised as the manifestation of forces and laws that flow into and out of our field of awareness, but which do not originate there.

4. The twenty-fifth path is imaged by the Tarot Atu Temperance XIV, which is also called Daughter of the Reconcilers: the Bringer-forth of Life. This is effectively the Guardian Angel or celestial intermediary between Man and God, Earth and Heaven. The magical power of the twenty-fifth path is called the Power of Transmutations. This owes to alchemy, typically the so-called transmutation of lead or iron, of the base substance into spiritual gold. Thus, the sacrifice of this path is here explained, for it is only dross that is relinquished.

ע

The Renewing Intelligence

1. The twenty-sixth path of A'ain connects Tiphereth, the sphere of the Sun, with Hod, the sphere of Mercury. The path is called the Renewing Intelligence.[46] It is so called because 'thereby God renews all the changing things that are renewed by the creation of the world' (Westcott). This refers to perpetual renewal of all manifested forms.

2. From the human or psychological point of view, the renewal refers to the adaptation that is required so the intellect does not atrophy— for the identification of the ego with the forms or constructs that appear in Hod increases the limiting or restricting power of Saturn, ruler of the zodiacal sign of Capricorn.

3. It is the desire to become free of material limitations that drives man to seek freedom, yet it is necessary to understand the principles of nature and their operation in the world before any limits can be transcended—the prime limitation being man, and his ignorance of spiritual and natural laws.

---

[46] ShKL MChVDSh (708).

4. The twenty-sixth path is imaged forth by Tarot Atu the Devil XV, which is also called Lord of the Gates of Matter: Child of the Forces of Time. The depictions of the 'Devil' are the distorted, monstrous representations of the pre-religious Goddess of life and love, for example Qutesh, Asherah or Ashtaroth.[47] The scarlet or golden girdle worn loosely about the waist of the Devil in the Marseilles Tarot was the signature of Asherah and other primal dancing goddesses. Note that 'Scarlet Woman' (AShH ShNI) counts to 666, a number often associated with Satan or the Antichrist, though it is also a symbol of the Sun and of Spirit, and therefore of Christ. The magical powers of the twenty-sixth path are the Witches Sabbath (so-called) and the Evil Eye. While the former symbolises the degraded remnants of long forgotten rites, the latter is the protection against the hostile forces thus unwittingly evoked.

ב

The Natural Intelligence

1. The twenty-seventh path of Pé connects Netzach, the sphere of Venus, with Hod, the sphere of Mercury. The path is called the Natural Intelligence, 'whereby the nature of everything found in the orb of the sun is completed and perfected'.[48] Westcott is probably more correct in saying 'the nature of everything *under* the orb of the sun'. (There is some confusion of the order of paths with Westcott, which has resulted sometimes in a mixing up of the twenty-seventh and twenty-eighth paths.)

2. On the ascent of this path there is a purgation by fire. Only thus may the voice of spiritual intuition be heard clearly above the tumult of mind. The power of Mars is the fluidic fire, comparable to the 'Voice of Fire' of the Chaldean Oracles, borne by the lightning flash with fulminating force. By this same power, the images or forms in Hod are ensouled—imbued with the substance of life and movement.

3. The work of the magician is to create such forms, for example talismans. It is the same power that is drawn down to consecrate and give life to such forms, which then form a permanent link between the practitioner and the non-human intelligences invoked.

---

[47] Crowley's *Thoth* Tarot *The Devil XV* is the exception to this. It would be unseemly to comment further in this place.
[48] ShKL MVTBO (899).

4. The twenty-seventh path is imaged forth by the Tarot Atu the Tower XVI, which is also called Lord of the Hosts of the Mighty. The magical powers of the twenty-seventh path are Works of Wrath and Vengeance, which refers to the powers of Mars.

צ

The Active Intelligence

1. The twenty-eighth path of Tzaddi connects Netzach, the sphere of Venus, with Yesod, the sphere of the Moon. The title of the path is the Active Intelligence.[49] It is called thus 'for thence is created the spirit of every creature of the supreme orb, and the activity, that is to say, the motion, to which they are subject'. The letter Tzaddi (fish hook) of this path is that of the holy king, specifically the fisher-king found in the lore of many traditions. This path is represented fairly by what is usually thought to be a 'crook and flail' carried by Egyptian kings; in fact, the 'crook' is more likely to symbolise an early form of needle for weaving, while the 'flail' is an instrument for threshing grain. Thus we have weaving and gathering on the one hand, and separation and purgation on the other, these being comparable to the dual and complementary principles of Peace and Justice.

2. The activity of this path, which stirs reflections as waves in the mirror of the Moon (the mind) gives rise in some to the delusion of instant enlightenment, that much can be gained spiritually in return for very little effort. The desire for acquisition of magical powers, or to be made healthy, wealthy and so forth, is no better than the urge for psychological improvement through hypnotism. All of that is the restless urge of the ego to maintain its tyranny over the soul through the perpetuation of ignorance, which mistakes the True Self (Atma) for all these contingencies.

3. Through inverse analogy, the Active Intelligence assumes the demoniacal forms of slavery and submission, especially when these are brought about by hypnosis, psychological or other manipulative means; all this is particularly pertinent in the technological age, where entire populations are controlled through helpless dependance on information and media for 'entertainment', to the extent that many will even feel 'educated and informed' by the very things that are keeping them in a state of constant delusion.

---

[49] ShKL MVRGSh (899).

4. The twenty-eighth path is imaged by the Tarot trump the Emperor IV, which is also called Son of the Morning: Chief among the Mighty. Lucifer or Satan, in Christian terms, is generally thought to be the 'son of the morning' referred to in the book of Isaiah, 14: 12, which is a title of Venus as the Morning Star. The title of the Tarot Atu is incorrectly given in Crowley's 'acquired' work, *Liber 777*, as *Sun* of the Morning. It is incorrect because the title refers to Venus, not the Sun. Chief Among the Mighty refers to the Golden Dawn placement of the trump on the fifteenth path from Chokmah to Tiphereth. Curiously, the title Son of the Morning better suits the change of placement to the twenty-eighth path of Tzaddi recommended in the (Egyptian) Book of the Law, I: 57. The magical power of the twenty-eighth path is that of Consecration, which owes to the fire of Aries.

ק

The Corporeal Intelligence

1. The twenty-ninth path of Qoph connects Netzach, the sphere of Venus, with Malkuth, the sphere of the visible universe. The title of the path is the Corporeal Intelligence.[50] It is named thus because it 'informs every body which is incorporated under all orbs, and it is the growth thereof'. It is concerned with the formation of all bodies as according to the revolutions of the Zodiac. The root of the word that is translated as 'corporeal' (*gosham*) implies a violent rainstorm or shower—the 'shower of the life of earth' that comes through the seed of the Bornless Spirit or Guardian Angel.

2. The 'seed' may here refer to the fluidic or formless fire from which all forms receive their essence. To understand the 'revolution of the Zodiac' and the part that it plays it is useful to know that the basis of the Zodiac is Spirit working through the Sun upon the four classical elements of Fire, Air, Water and Earth.

All bodies are composed of these elements, something that is in agreement in both Hindu and Hermetic source texts, although the terms used naturally differ. In Hinduism it is the *akasha* (spirit) that permeates all elements, and by analogy, this is the *purusha* or divine 'essence' by which substance is given.

3. The descent of this path is the embodiment of each creature, while the ascent of it implies knowledge of the 'essence' that informs all beings.

---

[50] ShKL MVGShM (739).

4. The twenty-ninth path is imaged forth by the Tarot Atu the Moon XVIII, and which is also called Ruler of Flux and Reflux: Child of the Sons of the Mighty. The magical powers of the path are said to be of Bewitchments and Casting Illusions. There is a note added to the translation of the *Book of Formation* to the effect, 'in black magic this path helps the operator to come *en rapport* with his victim'. It is important to understand that such 'black magic' is not in any way limited to the realm of traditional sorcery or ceremonial magick, but is used extensively in applications of psychological theories as well as in the works of some occult writers and fantasists.

ר

The Gathering Intelligence

1. The thirtieth path of Resh connects Hod, the sphere of Mercury, with Yesod, the sphere of the Moon. The path is called the Gathering Intelligence, 'for thence astrologers, by the judgment of the stars and the heavenly signs, derive their speculations and the perfection of their science according to the motions of the stars'.[51] The collecting of knowledge implied by the title is in the sense of a bringing to wholeness or perfection, thus it defines the Great Work. However, no amount of 'information' will accomplish any Great Work, so this does not imply the mere collection of data, as with the modern pseudo-astrology. Astrology here refers to traditional esoteric science, the starry wisdom, and has no more to do with the astrology of personal horoscopes than the esoteric knowledge of the Tarot has to do with professional psychics.

2. The Sun is the visible giver of light and life to the earth and all her creatures; it is by the solar lamp of the source of life itself that all knowledge is ordered by its principles. Without the solar intelligence, knowledge and facts serve no purpose other than to deepen delusion.

The gathering of disparate facts—facts from which nonsensical conclusions are drawn—typifies those lacking all positive qualities of the Gathering Intelligence. The heat of mental activity generated on this path must be guided by the Hermetic Light; it is the luminous lamp within that is kindled by steadfast work and meditation over a prolonged period of time.

---

[51] ShKL KLLI (440).

3. Every initiatic school of any worth incorporates some form of training of the mind. The two children depicted in some versions of the Tarot trump symbolise the dual solar and lunar principles in the soul. The path mirrors the twenty-eighth, the Active Intelligence that joins Yesod with the pillar of Force. Whereas the latter path confers the earnest desire to seek truth, the Gathering Intelligence guides by intellectual discrimination. It is only by rigorous discrimination that the right materials can be selected for the building of the Adytum.

4. The thirtieth path is imaged forth by the Tarot Atu the Sun XIX, which is also called the Lord of the Fire of the World. The magical powers attributed to the path are the alchemical Red Tincture and the Power of Acquiring Wealth. In ancient astrology, the Moon was understood to be the lens by which all other celestial powers exerted their influence upon the terrestrial domain. The magical power of the path connecting the Sun and the Moon is therefore that of acquiring wealth or gold—whether material or otherwise.

ש

The Perpetual Intelligence

1. The thirty-first path of Shin connects Hod, the sphere of Mercury, with Malkuth, the realm of Action and Elements, or visible universe. The path is called the Perpetual Intelligence.[52] It is so-called because 'it rules the movement of the sun and the moon according to their constitution, causing each to gravitate in its respective orb'. This path connects Malkuth with the left hand pillar of Form. The Perfect Intelligence of Hod is here realised 'in the flesh'. From the human point of view, the fruits of such knowledge come to pass as future events, though in reality there is only simultaneity. From the point of view of eternity there is no past or future; there is nowhere to go as eternity encompasses all—time as perceived in the earthbound sense simply ceases to exist.

2. Truth is eternally present and is the seed of each 'moment' in time—again, that is as seen from the strictly human perspective as time is not discontinuous, as are numbers. The perpetuity implied in the title refers to all states of manifestation. The 'wheel' of cyclical manifestation can be understood as two-sided; one side faces time while the other faces outside of time.

---

52 ShKL ThMIDI (814).

From yet another perspective, one side looks forward in time and the other looks backward. From the human perspective, time seems to pass by from 'moment to moment' so that we see a present that is moving forwards, with a past that is behind and a future in front.

3. The spiritual fire of this path is that which animates all living beings and is at the same time the 'seed' of the resurrection body as is formularised in the alchemical acronym INRI: *Igni Natura Renovata Integra*. This is quite often translated as 'The Whole of Nature is Renewed through Fire'. It might also be more accurately translated, 'Through fire, Nature is wholly restored to her integrality.'

4. The thirty-first path is imaged forth by Tarot Atu Judgement XX, which is also called Spirit of the Primal Fire. The traditional Tarot trump depicts the dead arising from their tombs in response to the vibration of the Angel of Judgment on the day of be-with-us. The Angel of the last trump is according to some Gabriel and to others, Israfel. The magical powers of the thirty-first path are Evocation and Pyromancy. These are derived from the correspondences of this path: firstly the trump, which depicts the dead arising from their graves (evocation), and secondly the element of fire (pyromancy).

ת

The Administrative Intelligence

1. The thirty-second path of Tav connects Yesod, the sphere of the Moon, with Malkuth, the realm of Action and Elements, or the visible universe. The title of the path is the Administrative Intelligence, 'because it directs all the operations of the seven planets, with their divisions, and concurs therein'.[53] The concurrence that is mentioned here is sometimes explained as 'partaking of the same nature', but that is only an appearance as a principle cannot have the same nature as that which is moved by it. Saturn brings all things to order, governance and form. In its inferior sense it equips the mind to know only of the mundane activities—work, survival and procreation.

2. On ascending the thirty-second path, this function is to a certain extent reversed and applied in an entirely different way: the man on the path of knowledge becomes conscious of processes that the average person is entirely unaware of. He must then consciously exercise the Saturnian discriminatory power or fall prey to every passing phantom—for this path is a passage leading to the lower astral or subtle plane.

---

[53] ShKL NOBD (476).

3. The inhabitants of the inferior limits of the subtle realm are very diverse; some are thought-forms that are not in any way intelligent in themselves but are detached or disembodied functions that are more or less automatic. This realm is thronged with ghosts—the discarded remnants of the dead—and graveyard ghouls, often mistaken for 'spirit guides' by those who trade in such things and which they, in their delusion, imagine to be 'higher spiritual forces'. There are also, especially in the realm of spiritism, a tendency to attract entities that are akin to those of *The Goetia*, and which they imagine to be human souls.

4. The thirty-second path is imaged forth by Tarot trump the World XXI, which is also called Great One of the Night of Time—depicted on most tarots as the world dancer or *anima mundi*, for the visible universe is but the shade of her beautiful luminosity. The magical powers of the thirty-second path are Works of Malediction and Death; also Alchemy, Geomancy and the Making of Pentacles. These are, as usual, derived from the correspondences of the path, Saturn and elemental earth.

THE PATHS
OF
EVIL

The Paths of Evil

According to the *Book of Formation*, good and evil exists in the hearts of men and so long as that state of affairs exists then there will always be an inversion of the divine intention. In the shadow of ignorance, when the shoots of a young tree are cut off from their root, their principle, there is only the Tree of Evil or of Death. This is illustrated in II: 4:

> Twenty-two basal letters: they are placed together in a ring, as a wall with two hundred and thirty-one gates. The ring may be put in rotation forwards or backwards and its token is this: Nothing excels ONG (pleasure) in good, and nothing excels NGO (plague) in evil.

In Hebrew, a word can take on several different meanings through its pronunciation as well as its spelling, as is the case with other sacred languages. The rearrangement of the letters may form a word with a different or even opposite meaning. The root GN means 'garden' or 'orchard', as in Garden of Eden.[54] It is from here that Adam 'fell', and from thereon the Tree of Life was inverted for him, and he was lost in its shadow. He can reclaim or restore it by his work (Sanskrit *karma*) or otherwise through devotion (*bhakti*) or knowledge (*jnana*). The two words ONG, 'good' and NGO, 'plague' (or evil), obviously have the same number 123 through their Qabalistic values, so at the same time are a Gematria equivalent. Similarly, the 231 gates mentioned in the text is a Qabalistic *temurah* or permutation of 123.[55]

It seems probable that a detailed development of inverse powers could not have come about until relatively modern times. The first ten paths and the twelve zodiacal paths thus have an infernal Order of Qliphoth or inverse hierarchy. As such, they really pertain to the Tree of Knowledge or Death, for the Qliphoth are a shadow inversion of the orders of angels, which are best understood as attributes of God, in the same way that in Hinduism the *devas* are powers or attributes of Mahadevi Shakti. All the names of angels end in El (אל), a name of God. It might seem odd then that many of the evil powers in Hebrew also end in the name of God. One should remember that nothing can exist without the divine principle. Thus, the 'Devil' and his ministers can only be an inverse reflection of God and his angels, which comes about through ignorance. Evil powers have no essential reality on their own ground and are barely within manifestation.

---

54 Garden of Eden = GN ODN.
55 $\sum (1–21) = 231$, a Pythagorean number.

Qliphoth of the Ten Sephiroth

1. The Order of the Qliphoth of Kether, the first path, is *Thumiel*, the Dual Contending Forces.[56] It may seem at first as though an Order of Qliphoth at the principial height of the Tree of Life is somewhat strange. It must be remembered that the inverse Tree is really that of Death, and that the implication, through reversing the natural order, is that all rule or governance is from *below*, not above. At the deepest and darkest level, the root of all ignorance is the divided self or ego. As Kether is essential unity, the inverse force is symbolised as two heads or contending forces masquerading as one. All duality really consists of complementaries, from the higher or principial point of view. It is only ignorance that sees pairs of oppositions.

2. The Order of Qliphoth of Chokmah, the second path, is *Ghagiel*, the Hinderers.[57] The idea conveyed is to hinder, to thwart or to otherwise impede the True Will. The word 'hinder' implies chasing, or an attack from behind, which is an inversion of the positive state of 'face to face with God'. In so far as Chokmah is at times identified, through satanic inversion, with the 'sexual force'—something that the psychological theorists since Freud have identified with *libido* or will—then it is curious that in Hebrew there is a word for 'unlawful' sexual congress when it is for physical pleasure only, and this can be translated as 'back to back'. This denotes the exclusion of love and it is interesting to see then how in popular culture 'love' is sometimes used as a word for sex, as in 'making love'.[58]

Such activity can harm the True Will when that is understood as the *dharma* or right orientation of an individual; sex is an intimacy that, no matter what the intentions of the persons involved, creates powerful links or bonds on the subtle as well as physical level. Compare with the Qliphoth of Netzach or Venus, where multiplicity creates confusion through the attachment to many objects of desire—objects that may have completely contradictory qualities; where the objects of desire are people, there is conflict of will.

---

[56] ThAVMIAL, 488.

[57] OIGIAL, 124.

[58] 'Making love' was at first a nineteenth century term for either courting or flirtation; since the twentieth century it was used to mean sex, regardless of whether love is involved or not. Thus 'love' is reduced to the purely physical level. It is curious that the Freudian notion of 'will' as *libido* also reduces the will to something belonging solely to instinct.

3. The Order of Qliphoth of Binah, the third path, is *Satariel*, the Hiders or Concealers of God.[59] Binah is the root of Form. It is also the domain of the Shekinah, the feminine holy presence, whose symbolism includes both the cloud and the rainbow. To be covered by such a cloud is the privilege of those that have reached the highest attainments in the initiatic traditions. Therefore the inverse aspect of Binah (and Saturn) is the concealing of the ineffable light by material illusion, which is ignorance. As a demonic power or attribute, this might be extended to the deliberate concealment of truth, or falsity in the most general sense. We might also include here the domain of the 'false prophets', those who are able to persuade others of their pure intentions, and where this is nothing but a mask of lies and conceit. As Saturn is the ruler of Aquarius, the precessional constellation of the present Age, the Hiders are those who pretend to reveal truth through scientism or other apparently rational means. In this sense, the Qliphoth of this path are the archetypical black magicians—not ritualists, but those who work tirelessly in the political or corporate domain to subvert the truth and impose falsity at all levels of society.

4. The Order of Qliphoth of Chesed or Gedulah, the fourth path, is *Gha'ashebelah*, Breakers-in-pieces or Smiters.[60] The inverse power of Chesed is injustice and malice, also destruction for its own sake. Chesed has a relation with the 'four', through its number, and so it has a relation with the Pythagorean decad.[61] While the Pythagoreans developed the geometry of such numerical symbolism, it belongs in vastly more ancient traditions such as that of the Hindus. The four Yugas or Ages are counted in reverse order: the first and longest Yuga, the 'Golden Age', is four. The last and shortest, the Dark Age, is counted as one. From the point of view of the first Yuga, it contains all three of the future Yugas and its form is spherical. From the point of view of the final Age of Kali, the form is a square, marking a completion of all possibilities of the first three and return through the great dissolution at the end of time (*mahapralaya*). The product of the four numbers is ten, the complete manifestation. The infernal agents that seek only to separate, destroy or break-in-pieces are thus in a certain sense the ministers of the System of Antichrist.

---

[59] SAThARIAL, 703.
[60] GOShBLH, 428.
[61] $\sum (1-4) = 10$.

♂

5. The Order of the Qliphoth of Geburah, the fifth path, is *Golachab*, the Flaming Ones.[62] The unrestrained, unbalanced force of Geburah or Mars here manifests in forms such as pyromania, unmitigated tyranny and destruction. The root *gola* (GVL) has many meanings but these include revolution or 'turning' and also shapelessness. Thus we have the thoughtless act, driven to extremes through a diabolical urge to change for its own sake, or otherwise vengeance. One thinks of the unrelenting horror of Shakespeare's *Titus Andronicus*. In the technological age, the mad fury of change for its own sake now presses on without any restraint; the motivation for this is seen as perpetual 'improvement' but in fact it is sheer greed arising from a social order, or social chaos to be more accurate, governed purely through economic needs that are in turn driven solely by numbers and quantity.

⊙

6. The Order of Qliphoth of Tiphereth, the sixth path, is *Tageriron*, the Hagglers, or Litigation.[63] Here we have contention and dispute arising from the illusion of the separateness of the ego: a divided self and will. The name is formed from the root word TGRN, 'to haggle or bargain'. The shadow of the Mediating Influence of Tiphereth is mere disruption and needless intervention. As with the previous fifth path, where change or destruction becomes completely mindless, the urge to provoke disequilibrium everywhere is similarly driven—and we should remember that Tiphereth is passive to the activity of Geburah.

We also have, in the present times, the fake ideal of 'unity' through uniformity. This automatically brings about contention and disharmony. Self-identity is now measured or 'proved' by numbers or digits, or otherwise by digital means. The selling of products through 'brands' has developed to an extent where consumers are proud to wear the logos or icons of the products on their clothing. The notion of corporate 'branding' started as something that served to identify the ownership of cattle but now serves to identify companies and individuals as part of a herd mentality. The legitimised herd are thus encouraged to imagine that by these tokens of emptiness they have something called 'individual self expression'.

---

[62] GVLChB, 49.
[63] ThGRIRVN, 869.

♀

7. The Order of Qliphoth of Netzach is *A'arab Zarq*, the Raven of Dispersion.[64] The raven is a bird of carrion, as opposed to the dove, which is the emblem of universal love that is attributed to Venus. Thus, the raven feeds on death, or on dead things. The unbalanced aspect of Venus is the dispersion of the will and mind that comes about through the insatiable pursuit of objects of desire, which are empty in themselves.

'Tearing oneself apart' is descriptive of the orgy of self-destruction that comes about through uncontrolled appetite. This is increased through sheer quantity or multiplicity. The modern world reduces love to mere sentiment and the spiritual to mere emotion or even 'lifestyle'. Only the body and senses are admitted to be in any way 'real'. The appearance of things is what counts, and the counting of money has by now become replaced by the collection of data by which artificial projections into the future are made, based on future profit. This has produced what is called a 'surveillance society', which invades everyone's privacy, or removes it altogether, and yet meets general approval as though it were a necessary evil. In the meantime, dispersion in media, 'entertainment' and so forth is now sold as though it were a positive quality, whereas in fact it only reflects the urge towards pure quantity, which will ultimately bring about the great dissolution at the end of time.

☿

8. The Order of Qliphoth of Hod is *Samael*, the Archdevil and False Accuser.[65] Hod is the eighth path of the Tree and is the sphere of concrete mentation, where the stream of force received from Netzach ensouls forms created by the mind. The 'accusations' then arise from a misplaced sense of identity that has been absorbed into an excess of conflicting ideas. The urge to accuse others of sin or error also stems from too much power received from Geburah along the watery twenty-third path; the judgements or severities are the lightning bolts of Jupiter and Mars that would otherwise burn up the dross of the personality through meditation. Here, the ego, unwilling to 'die' in this onslaught of fire and brimstone, looks instead for a victim, and having found a suspect is swift to assume the rôle of judge, jury and executioner.

---

[64] ORB ZRQ, 579.
[65] SMAL, 131.

Samael is sometimes viewed as the adversary of the Archangel Michael. Angels and devils often swap good and evil functions in different times and cultural traditions. Curiously, Samael is also the Genius of St. John according to some, and the protector of those who preach in foreign lands. St. John lived in the desert, a symbol of the primordial tradition. Lilith is often partnered as the consort of the archdemon (or angel) Samael. Lilith is the female embodiment of malice in one tradition, while in another she is the goddess of love. Note that the name Samael may also mean 'the North', and the 'Left-hand'. In some respects, Samael and Lilith can then be seen as comparable to Shiva and Shakti as they were known in Mesopotamia, Babylonia and the Middle East.

☽

9. The Order of Qliphoth of Yesod is *Gamaliel*, Obscene Ones or the Obscene Ass.[66] Gamaliel is also known as the 'Reward of God'. The demons are servitors of Lilith, considered as evil to some and holy to others; according to the Coptic *Revelation of Adam to His Son Seth*, Gamaliel is a celestial power or intelligence that has the specialised task of drawing initiates or 'chosen ones' upwards to heaven. It is the same power, in its inverse and most inferior form, that condemns souls to hell through submission to base instinct.

There is similarity between the Hebrew word for a mule or donkey and the Hebrew and Arabic word for a camel, *gimel*. Both are beasts of burden, so we might suppose that culturally such animals were regarded in a strictly utilitarian manner and as belonging to a lower order in the scheme of things, whereas the horse is always seen as having noble and indeed royal qualities. There is a suggestion that the different animals pertain to higher and lower castes. The hybrid nature of the ass then provides a clue, for it is a mixture of the noble caste and the lowest or servile caste. In Sanskrit, the word *shudra* for the menial caste includes the meaning of passion or desire. In the Talmudic saga the teacher and his student are riding on donkeys. When the student is permitted to expound on the divine chariot, the teacher gets off his donkey, sits on a stone under an olive tree and covers his head, lest the divine presence should visit them.[67] That is to say, he ceases his activity (*rajas*), holding the reigns of his senses, to take up a position of repose (*sattwas*). The olive tree and the stone are symbols of wisdom.

---

[66] GMLIAL, 114.
[67] Hagigah 14b. See 'The Hebraic Tradition'.

⊕

10. The Order of Qliphoth of Malkuth is *Lilith*, Woman of Night.[68] Lilith is one of four angels of sacred dance and love that are consorts of Samael, according to the *Zohar*. The four angels were originally Gods or Devas of sacred dance and oracular divination long before patriarchs abolished the rôle of the temple priestess. In biblical lore, Lilith was the first wife of Adam, before Eve. Lilith is comparable to the Babylonian Goddess Ishtar or Astarte. She is a personification of what is termed *prana* in the Hindu doctrines, which is divine breath, spirit or air. In that teaching, *prana* is no different from Brahma the supreme principle understood from the principial point of view.

As an unbalanced or demonic force, Lilith becomes the deceiver through appearances, comparable to Maya, although Maya is never given evil or demonic connotations in the Hindu doctrines other than that she deludes men through their ignorance of the true state of affairs. In the Judaeo Christian tradition, Lilith typifies everything that is truly abhorrent. As the Demon Queen of the Qliphoth, Lilith is sometimes also considered to be the bride of Satan.

Qliphoth of the Zodiac

♈

28. The Order of Qliphoth of the twenty-eighth path is *Ba'ariron,* the Flock.[69] A flock or herd symbolises the collective mind of the mob, temporarily united in a common instinct or desire that subsequently becomes magnified and reinforced. The twenty-eighth path of Aries is ruled by Mars and imaged by the Tarot key the Emperor IV. The ungoverned instincts have become the rulers of body and ego. The crowd is united in its ignorance and stupidity and gains a temporary strength from this.

The 'crowd' can also be a metaphor for ungoverned thoughts and desires. The Ram of Aries corresponds to the Lamb, the symbol of Christ and also Agni or Igni in the Hindu and other traditions. There are several accounts in the Gospels where Christ Jesus tires of the crowds of followers, condemns or curses them and withdraws into meditation. Curiously, politically minded persons that have sought to find something agreeable to them in Christianity have seen Jesus as a sort of 'man of the people', which is a complete inversion of truth.

---

[68] LILITh, 480.
[69] BOIRIRVN, 548.

♉

16. The Order of Qliphoth of the sixteenth path is *Adimiron*.[70] Usually this is given as 'Bloody Ones', although the root word ADVM means 'red' and the conjunction with M-IR implies 'angered' or 'embittered'. The sixteenth path conveys the blood or energy of wisdom to the opulent sphere of Jupiter. The inverse aspect is then the wasting of energy, perhaps giving rise to a vampirical force. The path is Taurus ruled by Venus, the adverse aspect of which is instability leading to lack of discipline and sure knowledge. Verbal communication is dependant on hearing correctly—there must be receptivity and attentiveness. 'Attention disorders', for example, stem from improper flow of energy—it is to pay attention to the *wrong things*; it is a misuse of energy or 'blood', which is a misdirection of the creative power of the imagination, of which the root is ignorant sexual practices.

♊

17. The Order of Qliphoth of the seventeenth path is here referred to *Tzelaladmiron*.[71] The Changers is the correct name for this path.[72] Shapeshifting, in this respect, is the degraded form of a traditional science. Modern day neo-spiritual practices led by witchdoctors with a psychology degree have reduced this to little more than fantasy but that does not mean that those seeking 'empowerment' might not succeed in evoking atavisms from the *sub-infra* or demonic levels of being, in which case they will not know or recognise this and they and their associates and families will have no means of protection against the forces unleashed.

The two words TzLLD and MIRVN are suggestive of a subversive rebellion of the will resulting in a failure to exercise intellectual discrimination. The adopting of different attitudes or points of view to please others is a well-known vice of Gemini. Gemini, Libra and Aquarius, the astrological triplicity of Air, may typify 'signs of the times' as we near the end of the Cosmic Cycle. The adopting of different points of view, denying that truth even exists so as to gain a temporary advantage, forms part of all postmodern studies. It is reflected in politics in Libra, and in collective humanity and in the global world order in Aquarius.

---

[70] ADIMIRVN, 321.

[71] TzLLD MIRVN, 460.

[72] This was wrongly given by Crowley as 'Clangers' in *777*. An unintentional irony, perhaps.

18. The Order of Qliphoth of the eighteenth path is *Shechariron*.[73] The name means the Black One. The eighteenth path is that of Cancer ruled by the Moon. The inference is to the extreme darkness of ignorance as opposed to the understanding that should be mediated on this path from Binah to Geburah. It is to act instinctively, as though in the dreaming state (symbolised by the Moon), without intelligent understanding. Vampirism corresponds to the inverse aspects of the eighteenth path, for the Holy Graal typifies the path. The drinking of blood, or the draining of the energy of another life, amounts to insatiable thirst for form—for example, the clinging to the body in the posthumous state.

Vampirism has become romanticised through popular fiction and yet Bram Stoker's novel *Dracula*, which was based on the tales of Nosferatu, portrayed the vampire as something truly horrible, that leads to indiscriminate feeding from any available matter that retains magnetism for the purpose of a prolongation of the subtle elements, or in other words, to cheat the 'second death'.

♌

19. The Order of Qliphoth of the nineteenth path is *Shalhebiron*, the Flaming One.[74] The nineteenth path of Leo connects the magnificent fountains of Jupiter with the fiery cauldrons of Mars. Unbridled lust is symptomatic of the inverse aspects of the path, also untrammeled egotism or egomania. The ancient Egyptian lioness goddess Sekhet is ascribed to this path as typifying sexual heat and fire. The inversion of the path comes about through succumbing to the powerful images or sounds (magnetic vibrations) that condense into a concentrated form outside the Gates of the Abyss and, through the magnifying intensity of the forces of Jupiter and Mars, become instantly 'alive'— there is a high risk of obsession. Leo is the opposite sign to Aquarius, and so is the occult power (in this case meaning literally concealed or invisible) of the present Age. The population become increasingly controlled in their behaviour at the same time remaining convinced that they are on the side of 'freedom' and a multitude of just causes. In the name of such idealism they will happily wipe out what is left of traditional culture and knowledge, replacing it with a parody of what it once was. The great secret (the occult part) is to know exactly who or what is really in control of all this.

---

[73] ShIChRIRVN, 784.
[74] ShLHBIRVN, 603.

20. The Order of Qliphoth of the twentieth path is *Tzaphiriron*, the Scratchers.[75] The sixth house in astrology corresponds to all small furry animals. One thinks of the persistent scratching of a rodent as akin to the erosion made upon the soul through the activity of the unregenerate ego—small-minded thoughts, wasteful and dispersive thoughts, thoughts of little consequence or import yet, when taken together, capable of thoroughly undermining and subverting the will.

The positive or solar aspects of the path relate to the True Will and knowledge of the cosmic purpose in all things. The distortion of this manifests in the unregenerate ego as the aimlessness and sense of futility that comes about through the dispersion of the mind: the inability to focus, the collecting of trivial or pointless facts for its own sake. In so far as the Hermit (or veiled Hermes) of the path knows how to Keep Silence, the afflictions of the inverse path of Virgo include logorrhoea.

♎︎

22. The Order of Qliphoth of the twenty-second path is *A'abiriron*.[76] The Clay Ones: the equilibrium of the universe requires Justice and Peace, as depicted by the eighth Tarot key Justice. Clay, on the other hand, is a thick, unwieldy substance that can nonetheless be used to sculpt forms. It is said that man or Adam was made from clay, since it is a red earth, like flesh and blood—the colour may also indicate the primordial tradition. Intellectual discrimination is required to perceive the operations of Justice and Peace, to perceive the divine in all things—which is never the things in themselves, but rather their principles. The man of clay, or of mud, divines little, knows nothing worth knowing, for he does not perceive any more than what his brute instincts tell him. The 'clay' here is the dark mud of ignorance and unknowing. As with the other two airy signs of the Zodiac, Libra typifies certain negative characteristics of the present and last Age of the Kali Yuga. As previously mentioned concerning the path of Nun, and which is also relevant here (see p. 42), the fake ideals of the Age include 'equality', which is only a cover for forcing everyone to be the same. 'Diversity' accomplishes much the same thing, for it pretends to allow differences but the allowance is conditional—those seeming differences must rigidly conform to the idealism that drives enforced uniformity in all things.

---

[75] TzPRIRVN, 636.
[76] OBIRIRVN, 548.

24. The Order of Qliphoth of the twenty-fourth path of Scorpio is *Nehesthiron*, Brazen One or Brazen Serpent (from *nahesh*).[77] The awakening and raising of the Serpent Power does not automatically bring wisdom. The twenty-fourth path connects Tiphereth, the centre of ego, with Netzach, the plane of desire. The unbalanced aspects therefore include the madness of a multiplicity of objects of desire leading to increasing states of delusion.

The mysteries of blood are associated with this path; in this case, it is the desire to continue a blood-line or lineage for physical self-replication—it is the delusion of mistaking the Self (Atma) for the objects of desire, such as children, posterity, fame, etc. The begetting of future generations is everyman's token of immortality yet it is no more than that—a medium of exchanging one thing for another. In this case the knowledge of the eternal life is exchanged for death and the perpetuation of the state of ignorance. Perpetuity through future generations is illusionary for the ego is not immortal; one drop of blood is in fact very much like another.

♐

25. The Order of Qliphoth of the twenty-fifth path is *Neheshiron*, the Snakey One.[78] The twenty-fifth path connects the Sun and Moon; its letter *samekh* means 'a prop', a support or crutch—a term that is sometimes use as a euphemistic allusion to the junction where the legs join the torso in the human body. The shape of the letter itself forms a cave, a symbol of the centre of the self or heart of Brahma. The word 'cave' also declares silence over the mysteries. However, it is the inversion that we are concerned with here, so the sealed off enclosure is the belief in the separate ego identity and the kind of silence is only that which serves to cover a lie.

The Arrow of Sagittarius is in some respects the Kundalini or Serpent Power. The inverse of the Guardian Angel is the Evil Genius, where the ego works 'undercover', or in a way that is not realised by the person, invoking self-deception, pride and vanity. It is easily possible to misinterpret the 'trials and ordeals' that correspond with the necessary sacrifice, in which case the aspirant turns aside from the path feeling betrayed, victimised or trapped by fate.

---

[77] NChShThIRVN, 1,024.
[78] NChShIRVN, 624.

Idealism in all shapes and forms begets self-righteousness, fuelled by the hot pursuit of self-born causes. Through self-identification the idealist becomes enslaved. Such causes may seem quite reasonable, especially the more benign ones such as vegetarianism, but in such cases the cause, while seemingly rational, comes with a host of more sinister or subversive attachments that place an impassable barrier between the aspirant and any real spiritual knowledge, apart from the self-identification that is inevitably involved: if food is *prana* and *prana* is Brahma from the principial point of view, then rejection of any particular food amounts to the rejection of the Real in one of its manifestations. In the postmodern world, the 'particularity' involved with such things can easily reach levels of actual insanity. Sannyasins were thus instructed to eat any sustenance that was offered them, and be thankful for it. The Sannyasin is left free to discriminate that which is not the Real, the Atma; for to be concerned with egoistic idealism is to remove the power of right discrimination and so to sink into delusion from which escape might not be possible.[79]

♑

26. The Order of Qliphoth of the twenty-sixth path is *Dagdagiron*, the Fishy One.[80] The astrological glyph for Capricorn is a goat with a fishes tail. The fishy tail is a reminder that the Zodiac signs are best understood in pairs; the watery sign of Cancer is the opposite in the Zodiac to that of Capricorn. The Tarot key for the twenty-sixth path is the Devil XV—material illusion veiling the Hermetic Light. The path connects Hod, the sphere of mentation on the Form side of the Tree, with Tiphereth, the radiant centre of all. When the ego invests the power of belief in the names and forms it has created, identifying with them, the objects themselves enslave the soul.

The abuse or misdirection of generative power begets monstrous forms on the most inferior level of the astral plane. The magnetic power of such forms easily lends itself to obsession. The inversion of the path therefore includes every kind of fear-phantom that arises in the reactionary ego. By clinging on to the constructs of mind that are necessarily incomplete and imperfect expressions of their true forms, the tyrant becomes bound to the hideous, distorted forms of his own imagining, which then become endlessly multiplied and reflected in the world of that individual. These will of course be seen reflected in the thoughts and actions of others.

---

[79] Needless to say, political attachments and the like also produce nothing but hypocrisy when combined with a pretence to spiritual knowledge.
[80] DGDGIRVN, 280.

≈

15. The Order of the Qliphoth of the fifteenth path is *Bahimiron*, the Bestial One.[81] When the dissolution of the ego implicit on this path (as Aquarius) is resisted but the force remains irresistible—the momentum too great to overcome—then there is a reversion to type. The return to the True Self manifests in its degraded form as loss of consciousness in bestiality or sexual perversion—an attempt to annihilate the self in the undifferentiated state.

It should be understood then that there is a lower form of the undifferentiated 'primal chaos' and a higher form of the unmanifest. Viewed as two axial poles, the higher is the principial state, and marks a return to that state, which is the goal of yoga for example. The lower is merely a reduction to base elements culminating in total disappearance. Occultists have unknowingly or deliberately confused this, blurring the difference or in some cases denying all spiritual possibilities as 'non-existence'. The precessional Age of Aquarius of the present time happens to coincide with the ending of the Age of Kali Yuga, the last Age in an entire Cosmic Cycle. Such deliberate obscurity is a characteristic of the times.

The failing ego may also seek refuge in collective consciousness, finding a temporary strength in the pose or attitude of the crowd, the approval of a peer group. The fifteenth path crosses the Abyss: 'By his knowledge the depths are broken up, and the clouds drop down the dew' (Proverbs, 3: 20). The inferior or inverse aspect of this is simple ignorance of all spiritual things and the obscurity of Darkness.

♓

29. The Order of the Qliphoth of the twenty-ninth path is *Shimiron*, Malignant Women.[82] The twenty-ninth path connects Venus, the lowest sephira on the Force side of the Tree, with Malkuth, the dead-end of matter. The women of malicious intent are the phantasms of decaying (or thwarted) desire, rife with poisoning and corruption. As such, these 'women' are no more than blind forces, but they have a tremendous capacity to inflict harm on the unwary human. 'Hell hath no fury like a woman scorned' is an aphorism that can apply not only to the human but also to the elementar that has been deprived of 'blood' or energy (compare with the other two watery signs, Cancer and Scorpio).

---

[81] BHIMIRVN, 323.
[82] ShIMIRVN, 616.

By analogous transposition, the intelligence of the twenty-ninth path orders the neural and biological patterns that in turn influence the behaviour of species, whether these are supposed to be 'sentient' or otherwise. When the human ego identifies itself personally with the biological urge to procreate or self-replicate—that great force which is, as a matter of fact, an entirely impersonal one—all manner of psychological or mental aberrations occur. For example, a person may seek self-fulfilment in the production of offspring; when they find the result is nothing of the sort they may subvert or redirect the flow of life-force into other objects of desire.

Typical afflictions arising from this are eating disorders, so-called—for devouring and begetting are the dual principles of the Great Mother at the cosmic level. The predatory behaviour of both men and women, especially when it forms part of a group mentality, is another, less specific. Alcoholism is yet another trait, since it arises from a desire to be reabsorbed back into the stream of life from whence the organism was formed. Yet it is the self-assertion of the ego—maintaining the primary delusion that it has a separate life and existence of its own—that is the root of all ailments of the soul.

THE 'NIGHTSIDE' TUNNELS OF SET

Satanic Inversion of the Paths

Our involvement with the 2014 revised edition of the book *The Nightside of Eden* was to check and correct Kenneth Grant's Gematria on Hebrew, Greek and other terms. This enabled us to gain an intimate understanding of how Grant used the deliberate inversion of symbolism to totally eliminate all spiritual possibilities for those who would follow him. That work also made it possible for us to discover the Hebrew spellings of the Genii of the Qliphoth of Aleister Crowley's *Liber 231*, which is the subject of *Nightside*, and which until then was a 'mystery' as only the Qabalistic numbers were given. Grant called these inverse paths the Tunnels of Set, as part of a 'Typhonian Tradition', although no such tradition exists. There was a Setian Gnosis within hermeticism and a cult of Set in ancient Egypt, but Grant's work, culled from diverse sources, is fantasy. A tradition cannot be self-invented. *Liber 231* is attributed to Crowley; however, the latter is known for his plagiarisation of the work of others so we cannot know for sure. *Liber 231* is no more than a list of names with brief descriptions and small drawings, presumably by Crowley. In the ferment of Grant's macabre imagining, this was expanded into the twenty-chapters of the second section of *Nightside of Eden*. Grant was exclusively interested in the qliphotic aspect of the paths.

What is perhaps unique to Western occultism, or was once unique at least, as the Western mentality has now become 'global', is the inversion of symbolism so that the higher or spiritual meaning is lost altogether, or as is very often the case, deliberately denied. This gives rise to that which we term as 'satanism'. The term is subject to much misunderstanding so it should be understood in the present context to refer to the deliberate, subversive inversion of symbolism.

Grant was candid in admitting that he had no knowledge of, or even any interest in, any spiritual path whatsoever, or in any kind of teaching. For example, the purpose of his book *At the Feet of the Guru* was to deal exclusively with supernatural phenomena produced by notorious gurus. The main subject of interest was in magical tricks and 'extraordinary' manifestations—something that always fascinates neo-spiritualists. In some ways it might be said that he used similar devices in his writing, deluding his followers with the ambiguous inversion of all traditional symbolism gathered from a wide variety of sources, along with extensive elements of fantasy produced from his own imagination or from the writing of others, whether fiction or non-fiction.

71

Using the terms of Advaita Vedanta, Grant made it appear as though the Supreme Realisation of the Self as Brahma, as taught by Shankaracharya for example, could be obtained by conjurations of demonic forces, with the added assistance of sexual magick and voyeuristic onanism. It may seem surprising but many persons have been taken in by this subterfuge, to the extent they even think that Grant was a kind of 'teacher' or guru in his own right—something that he would have laughed at and mocked, since he never pretended to be any such thing! Grant could, perhaps, be considered as one of the first postmodern occultists, with whom there is no truth but 'what you make of it'.

It only remains to be added that some of these entries contain more or less explicit references to actual practices of a very degraded type, and that anyone attempting them will certainly 'reap what they sow' in due course, by which time it will be far too late to annul the direful repercussions. Grant managed to convince many persons that evocation of the Qliphoth, and in a very informal manner at that, might actually be a means of gaining 'enlightenment' or some kind of 'initiation'. Sadly, this started a fashionable trend so that it is now not at all uncommon to hear of deluded persons evoking the seventy-two demons of *The Goetia* on a nightly basis for gain, profit, or in the hope of learning some 'occult secret'. Books have been published by ignorant persons that think it is only a matter of psychology, and that 'it's all in your head' and so no harm can come of evoking evil forces deliberately. Our purpose in presenting extracts from the *Nightside of Eden* is to show how those who develop an unnatural fascination with evil invariably become the puppets of the infernal forces they so vainly imagine they can control. Grant's inversion of symbolism, to the exclusion of all spiritual meaning, is a fine example (if we can use such a term) of satanism; it shows the diabolical consequences on those who propagandise it in their writing as much as on those who take it seriously enough to put it into practice.

The names of the twenty-two Genii of the Qliphoth are from *Liber 231*, Aleister Crowley, the 'very sinister' book that was the subject of Kenneth Grant's *Nightside of Eden*, Part Two.

א △

11. The satanic inversion of the eleventh path is here referred to *Amprodias*, the Genius of the Qliphoth of the path.[83]

> The sigil of Amprodias exhibits a gaping mouth typical of the uterus which utters the Word. This Word is the Hidden Light, the symbol of which is the whirling cross or swastika. It is identical with the letter A or *aleph*, the letter attributed to the eleventh path.

[Grant goes on to point out that the magical power of the path is divination:]

> This depends upon the divine or supra-mundane aspect of spirit that rays into the womb and fecundates the virgin earth with Light (intelligence) from beyond the ultimate Pylon (Kether). Divinatory power is the intuitive aspect of intelligence and as such its course is unpredictable as the forked lightning which cleaves the womb of space and manifests as the thunderbolt—the A between the I and the O.

[And furthermore, that the leaking or wasting of blood or vital energy produces the sylph-like phantoms of this path:]

> This breeds phantoms that appear in the form of sylphs; elementals associated with air or aethyr. Like the fairies and spirits of childrens' tales they are, more often than not, depicted as diaphanous and beguiling creatures. But in the aspect in which they manifest on the negative side of the Tree, they haunt the awful chasms of inner space where they appear in semblances of utmost horror which obsess the magician and sometimes drive him literally out of his mind. They then invade the vacated space and, like leeches, drain the blood of the mind into their own organisms.

To say that divinatory power is the "intuitive aspect of intelligence" is to mistake intellectual intuition for something that pertains to an inferior plane to that of real intuition. Lightning and the thunderbolt are symbols of initiatic transmission but to liken these to the 'course taken by divination' reduces them to a kind of chaotic state of affairs that can take only place within the human psyche, especially if in the trance-like condition so liked by psychic mediums.

---

[83] AMPRVDIS, 401.

It is nonetheless certainly true that the leaking of blood or vital energy may produce sylph-like phantoms. The 'awful chasms of inner space' refers really to the inferior chaos of the undifferentiated state, which, as we shall see, in spite of Grant's warnings, is the state that he seems to want to encourage the foolish magician to enter.

ב ☿

12. The satanic inversion of the twelfth path is referred to *Baratchial*, the Genius of the Qliphoth of the path.[84]

According to Grant, Baratchial is a reflection and inversion (in the Tunnels of Set) of Tiriel, the Intelligence of Mercury. The 'hidden' nature of the path is that of a dark priest—this was drawn from the Gematria equivalents to the number 260.[85] Grant maintains a difference between a black magician—which in his writings refers to his notion of a priest of Set—and the 'Black Brother' as was posited by Aleister Crowley. The Black Brother has shut himself up in his ego and, in order to preserve his self-identity against the 'inertia of the universe', becomes a vampire, requiring a ready supply of victims to preserve him. If it seems hard to see a difference between the latter and the former, which is Grant's own idea of a dark priest, then that is because there is no difference in effect! Vampirism was in fact a preferred method of Grant.

> This [duality] is evidenced by the symbols of Baratchial: two swords with inturned blades, suggesting intense concentration on the ego as opposed to the Self of All, flanking a ghostly face (mask) surmounted by a crescent moon. The sigil is a glyph of falsity and illusion reflected in the current of duality that reveals the Shadow of Thoth in the image of his ape or cynocephalus.

> The Black Brother is double tongued, as the serpent, which is significant, for the magical power [of the path] is the Gift of Tongues, the Gift of Healing, and a Knowledge of the Sciences. The healing here however is the healing of the ego, which merely aggravates with illusion the disease of false identity creating thereby a chain of endless suffering. Likewise, the Sciences of which knowledge is given are the sciences of darkness. Yet it must not be supposed that these are necessarily evil, it is merely that in the hands of a Black Brother they necessarily tend to sterility because directed towards the fulfilment of wholly personal ambitions.

---

[84] BRTChIAL, 260.
[85] TMIRA, 'hidden', and KMR, 'blackness' or 'priest', are both equal to 260.

The dark sciences of this path contain the secrets of the *kalas* of the void, and of that Kalinian Current which obtains in the widdershins world of anti-light. The witches and wizards of this tunnel speak with 'voices' that are reflected into the aura of the Adept by the mechanism of unnatural acoustics associated with the mysterious ventriloquism of Bath Kol, the Voice of the Oracle. The *bath* or *beth* is the house or womb of the supreme *kala*, and of the source of that ventriloquism that was primal in the myths of man, for the Word was endowed with flesh and issued from the belly of the mother. Here again, the number of Baratchial, 260, corroborates the doctrine of this path of *beth* for it is the number of MINMOM, 'pleasures', 'delights', and of IRKIK, 'thy thighs', which reveals the sexual nature of these pleasures.

This particular *kala* shows clearly how the face of the Tree is—and can only be—a façade. This is so because [it is] a reified and therefore dualistic interpretation of the hidden currents of energy that pulse through the tunnels on the other side of the Tree [to] transmit the energies of Non-being.

Once again, Grant displays quite a gift of the 'forked tongue' himself when he pretends that infernal or demonic forces can somehow lead a person to spiritual knowledge of the True Self (Atma). Here we have confusion between the 'energies of Non-being'—a very strange contradiction in terms as that which does not exist clearly cannot be an 'energetic force'—and the unmanifest principle of supreme reality that is the complement of the manifest at the level of Pure Being.

$$\text{ג } \text{☽}$$

13. The satanic inversion of the thirteenth path of Gimel is referred to *Gargophias*, the Genius of the Qliphoth.[86] According to Grant,

The magical powers of the *kala* of the moon include clairvoyance and divination. Not the kind of divination associated with the eleventh *kala* which issues ventriloquially via the open womb, but divination by dreams emanating from the 'sealed womb at night', i.e. when the lunar light is eclipsed.

The menstrual incense of the 13th *kala* assumes the forms of lemures ... the term connotes more than the ghosts of the departed, for the 13th tunnel is haunted by the ape-like teratomas spawned upon the 12th path which seep into the lunar miasma via the sleep of the virgin.

---

[86] QRGGPZ, 393.

The fluid plasma of the astral light that permeates the tunnels [of Set] is alive with potential that becomes manifest only when it comes to the surface of the Tree, splits into myriad forms, and swarms through the black hole in space represented by Daath, the Gateway to the Abyss. The manifestation of the non-manifest is effected, magically speaking, via the lunar current which characterizes the High Priestess of this *kala* in her virginal, unawakened, or 'dreaming' phase.

Here Grant exercises his preoccupation concerning menstrual blood, imagining that entrance into the undifferentiated state at the most inferior level of the subtle plane can somehow facilitate what it is otherwise the goal of yoga to accomplish. According to the Vedanta, this kind of *prakriti* is no different from 'ignorance'. The notion of 'fluidic plasma' was the peculiar invention of the nineteenth century occultists, especially the Theosophical movement and those who were influenced by them. It bears no relation to any ancient doctrine. Again, the notion of Da'ath as a 'black hole in space' owes to a similar kind of invention based on popular scientism.

ד ♀

14. The satanic inversion of the fourteenth path of Daleth is referred to *Dagdagiel*, the Genius of the Qliphoth of the path.[87] According to Grant,

Her qabalistic attribution is Daleth, meaning 'a door'; the door that permits of access to her house or womb, and egress from it. Her cosmic power-zone is Venus. This tunnel backs the first Reciprocal Path on the Tree of Life; its infernal counterpart is the base of the pyramid which, when inverted, is balanced upon the point of the Ain in the void of the Abyss—for this reciprocal tunnel is reflected into the gulfs beyond Kether.

The magical power corresponding to this *kala* is, traditionally, the ability to distil love philtres. The phrase is a euphamism for the vaginal vibrations emanating from the virgin in the form of sexual magnetism that attracts the Creative Light into her womb.

The virgin thus becomes the whore, or, in the language of magical symbolism, the entranced priestess becomes enlightened or awakened; the pythoness becomes oracular, being inspired with the divine spirit.

In the tunnel underlying the 14th path the [spider's] web is not structured from a plane surface but occupies various planes so that—from the point of view of an observer working upon this path—the criss-cross filaments produce a crazy geometry.

---

[87] DGDGIAL, 55.

From within the tunnel, and viewed from behind the Tree, however, the web is seen to form with infinitely tenuous threads of gossamer light the curious apertures of darkness that admit to gulfs of space between the back and front of the Tree. At the midmost depth of this tunnel the primal magical spell was cast and the first of all magical circles (webs) was formed.

Here is a spectacular display of both confusion and symbolic inversion. If Da'ath is the apex of an inverted tetrahedron, of which the supernal sephiroth are the base, then that 'point' can only touch on an inverted or mirror form of the Ain. It is impossible for this to be reflected into the 'gulfs beyond Kether', unless we see this as the *sub-infra* realms below the level of manifestation—and therefore on a sub-human level as opposed to a supra-human level. In fact, it is this *sub-infra* domain that all of Grant's work alludes to, though he pretends it has something to do with the Advaitan path of the non-dual. When Grant refers (in the third paragraph quoted) to the pythoness being "inspired by the divine spirit" we know he is joking; this is meant to be the demonic aspect of the path.

ה ≈

15. The satanic inversion of the fifteenth path is *Hemethterith*, the Genius of the Qliphoth.[88] According to Grant,

> The letter assigned to both Mother and Daughter is Hé, the number 5, and the Pentagram is her seal. The two waters are respectively the blood of the virgin daughter and the milk of the enceinte mother.

> Aquarius plays a vital rôle in the symbolism of the New Aeon. It is the place of the North attributed to Nuith who brings forth the two waters depicted in the sign of Aquarius as two undulating lines.

> In the Tarot Trump attributed to this sign a woman is seen pouring the waters from two jars. The seven-pointed Star of Venus above her is identical with the seven-rayed Star of Babalon, the Seal of Set which comprises the Mother and Child in one glyph ... these stars or rays were the seven heads of the Dragon of the Deep that later appeared in the Christian myth [*sic*.] as the Beast of the Apocalypse. The Star of the 15th *kala* is therefore the Star of Sothis or Shaitan, and it is concealed in the feminine generative essence known as the soul or blood of Isis.

> The stellar energy that flashes its light through this tunnel is symbolized by the Dog Star, Sothis, and the nature of the child born in this cell of Hemethterith is satanic in the sense that it is procreated by a magical method involving the use of the Eye of Set.

---

[88] HMThTRTh, 1,054.

The notion of a 'New Aeon' is of course a fantasy of Aleister Crowley. At best, it could refer to the incoming precessional Age of Aquarius but that was not what Crowley had in mind. Grant's equation of one symbol with another symbol tells us absolutely nothing about the symbolism; but whatever the seven-rayed star is supposed to be, he wants us to think that it has something to do with vaginal fluids, which, according to him, is what all symbolism alludes to! In this, Grant is always consistent: he reduces all symbolism to the gross or material level, as though that is an explanation of its meaning. As for the 'soul of Isis', that is something that Grant was clearly unqualified to speak of.

The "magical method involving the use of the Eye of Set" refers to an operation by a priest and priestess during an eclipse of the Moon for 'works of materialization and reification'.[89] By the 'eclipse of the Moon' Grant means here the onset of menstruation; he was very interested in the use of blood as a means of evoking infernal forces. Grant is for once being truthful when he confesses that the products of his magical method are 'satanic'.

ﬧ ﬡ

16. The satanic inversion of the sixteenth path is referred to *Uriens*, the Genius of the Qliphoth.[90] According to Grant,

> The name Uriens suggests Oriens, who, as Atlas, supported the universe on his shoulders. The idea of support or bearing is borne out by the general symbolism associated with this *kala* which endows the Adept with the magical *siddhi* of physical strength. The magical instrument ascribed to the 16th path is the Seat, Throne, or Altar, which are curiously feminine symbols for a *kala* associated with *The Hierophant* until it is remembered that, in the New Aeon, the 'Lord Initiating' (i.e. the Hierophant) is the god Set, who is identical with his Mother, Typhon, and therefore the continuation—as has been shown—of her *kala*, 15. She is in fact the Goddess 15, a name given to the Woman Fulfilled whose symbol, the full moon, occurred on the 15th day. The 16th *kala* was therefore her child, i.e. Set, and Set-Typhon under a single image was typified by the Dog Star, Sothis. According to Wilkinson [*The Ancient Egyptians*], Set-Typhon was known as 'The Giant' and this symbolism equates it with the pre-eval Nephilim.

---

[89] *Nightside of Eden*, Part Two, Chapter 9.
[90] ORIHNS, 395.

Within the inverted dimension of these spaces stands the Throne of Samael. Before this stands the altar on which is stretched the nocturnal Lilith, Mother of Abortions. The concept is explicit in the number of Uriens, for 395 is MShKLH *Abortiens*. Furthermore, the reflection of the Hierophant is refracted into the depths of the Abyss in the form of Set or Pan (Samael), the devil or double being the 'opposite' image. Likewise, this concept is explicit in the number of Uriens, for 395 is MShNH, meaning 'twofold', 'duplex'. It derives from the Egyptian *shen*, 'two', 'twofold circle', and 'the other', the alter ego.

Thus are the Heavens (HShMIM = 395) reflected into the hells, and the Hierophant or Magus of the Eternal becomes the Judge of the 'dead', whose symbol is the jackal, the howler in the haunts of the dead, and the 'eater of dung in the day of Be With Us'. At the termination of this abominable repast the Adimiron (The Bloody) swarm across the desolate places of the void leaving the 'rich brown juice' of annihilation in their wake.

Grant always used the Sanskrit term *kala* or *kalas* in a very general sense, to mean any kind of 'emanation' or even a 'colour, shade or hue', for example. In Sanskrit the meanings of this word are manifold but it is also very specific, depending on how the word is spelled and pronounced. Grant here accepts the description of the magical power of the sixteenth path as 'physical strength', which is a gross limitation especially as all magical powers so-called (or *siddhis*) really pertain to the subtle realm. In any case, any person so endowed would more likely be a sideshow attraction at a fun fair or circus than any kind of 'Adept'. The 'Goddess 15' is something that owes exclusively to the invention of Kenneth Grant but refers to the full Moon. We can only wonder at the meaningless confabulation of symbolism that follows: Set is identified with Sirius, which is reasonable enough but he is then thrown in with the biblical race of Nephilim as though simply putting the two things together might mean something.

In the second paragraph Samael, a Hebrew or Semitic angel or otherwise archdemon, is confused with the Greek god Pan as though the equation was a matter of fact. It seems this is mainly an excuse to indulge in fantasies based on the old cliché of the priestess spread out naked on an altar waiting to be 'sacrificed'. Grant's etymology is nearly always suspect; any link between the Hebrew MShNH and Egyptian *shen* is simply invented to fit the 'narrative'. The Hebrew word *mishnah* actually means 'repetition' and is used to refer to the traditional sacred texts written down from the oral tradition. The psychological notion of an 'alter ego' has nothing to do whatsoever with the Egyptian *shen* ring hieroglyph. The final paragraph speaks for itself.

17. The satanic inversion of the seventeenth path is here referred to *Zamradiel*, the Genius of the Qliphoth.[91] According to Grant,

> His number is 292, that of TzRB, 'the raven', the black bird of Set. TzRB also means 'evening'; at sunset the raven commences its predatory flight. BTzR, a metathesis of TzRB, signifies 'gold', the metal assocociated with the twins Set-Horus, Set's totem being the black bird and that of Horus the golden falcon. The earlier twins, however, were Set and Anubis, the golden jackal who, with his dark shade, haunted the desert of mummies, i.e. the astral shells left by those who had made the crossing and transcended the abyss.

> This tunnel concentrates the influence of Set via the Black power-zone (Binah) that receives its light from the Stellar Sphere (Chokmah) and rays it downward through the abyss. The 17th *kala* is thus strongly charged with the atmosphere of Daath and of Death, both of which have close affinity with the Lovers.

> The number 292 is also that of Chozzar which is probably connected with the name Choronzon, a corrupt form of it. The symbol of Chozzar resembles the astrological sign of Neptune. It is the symbol of Atlantean Magic and its attribution to the second power-zone, Chokmah, is highly significant because Chokmah receives an influx directly from Pluto (Kether).

> Chozzar means 'a pig'. This creature was adopted as a symbol of the Great Work by the Typhonians because it was the only animal known to devour human excrement. The pig is symbolic and so is the excrement, for it is not anal refuse that is veiled by this totem, but the blood of the moon, the human female flux in its dark phase.

> The imbibation of the black wine of the moon prepared the initiate for the disintegration, or crucifixion, at Easter time, and this made possible the crossing-over into the world of spirit or Non-being. The Gnostics depicted Chozzar in the form of a Serpent whose stellar representative was Draco. The undulation of the serpent was an image of the periodic feminine flow. It is from this tunnel [of Set] that dark forces emerge and seep from the abysses of non-being, permeating the power-zones of manifestation with the shadows of their absence. This doubling or dappling with light and shade is typified by symbolic hybrids such as the magpie, the penguin, the piebald, the parrot, the zebra; in fact, all dappled and chameleon-like creatures that have the apparent power of transformation.

---

91 ZAMRDIL, 292.

Those who truly 'cross the abyss' do not leave behind any 'astral shells'—an idea that was in any case invented by the Theosophists. The notion that the symbol of Neptune also symbolises 'Atlantean Magic' is pure fantasy, as is most of this incoherent and indeed quite revolting mix of the fantastical and the absurd. Once again we find that 'the world of spirit' is confused with 'Non-being', by which Grant can only mean dispersal in an undifferentiated and inferior state.[92]

ה ♋

18. The satanic inversion of the eighteenth path is *Characith*, the Genius of the Qliphoth.[93] According to Grant,

> Cancer is the astro-glyph of the Holy Graal and 640 is the number of KVS ThNChVMIM, the Cup of Consolation; and that which consoles the Adept on the Path of Cheth is the Graal of Our Lady. Such is the nature of this Chalice which yields both ecstasy and magical immortality that its *kalas* are highly addictive. Should the Adept linger over long in this tunnel the addiction becomes obsessive and he runs the risk of becoming a vampire, draining cup after cup of the hellbroth distilled by the Great Harlot, the Mother of Abominations, who yields eagerly to the dark desires of those who are drunk on the wine of her fornications.

> The magical formula of this *kala* is cunnilinctus which, if it exceeds the proper limits leads not only to the death [by depletion] of the partner but also of the magician himself. The Order of Qliphoth inhabiting the tunnel of Characith is therefore known as the Shichiririon, 'the Black'. When the sun reddens or sets he is said to be drinking the blood of the goddess or 'performing the higher form of cunnilinctus'.

> The number of Characith, 640, is also that of ShMSh, the Sphere of the Sun, which equates with MMSK (640), meaning 'a drink offering', and ThMR the 'palm of the hand' and a 'palm tree'. The dates of the palm tree are connected with the phenomena of menstruation.

The palm tree in fact symbolised peace in Mediterranean countries, and its fruits prosperity. No 'Adept', in any case, would be exploring the Tunnels of Set such as were imagined by Kenneth Grant. The repetitious themes of the latter are clearly evident of the obsessions written about working on the author, himself the helpless victim of the infernal forces he spent his whole life evoking imaginatively.

---

[92] Even when non-being is referred to the higher principle, Advaita is clear that being and non-being are still attributes and so do not in any way constitute the supreme reality.

[93] ChARAKITh, 640.

ט ♌

19. The satanic inversion of the nineteenth path is *Temphioth*, the Genius of the Qliphoth.[94] According to Grant,

> The number 610 is that of AThRVG, meaning 'lust' and 'desire'. This is in accord with the Tarot Trump entitled *Lust* relevant to the Path above this tunnel. The trump shows a woman mounted upon a leonine beast with seven heads: 'The head of an Angel: the head of a Saint: the head of a Poet: the head of an Adulterous Woman: the head of a Man of Valour: the head of a Satyr: and the head of a Lion-Serpent' [*Book of Thoth*, Crowley]. Another form of 610 is ChBRTh which means 'coupling point', 'place of conjunction', and it is in the tunnel of Temphioth that the magical coupling of the woman and the beast occurs. This is confirmed by the image of KPhRTh (610), the 'mercy seat', and 'place of the two cherubs', originally known as the place or house of the two beetles, such being the sign of Khephra. On the 19th path the lioness Sekhet is the vehicle of the force of Leo, which she represents as the torrid summer sun at its zenith, this being typical of sexual heat.
>
> Sekhet is the sexual heat of Isis, the force that overcomes 'evil'. It is shown by her bridling the Beast whereon she rides.
>
> The Order of Qliphoth ascribed to this tunnel is the Shalchbiron or The Flaming; the flames that lick the cauldron of the Sabbath in which the lion-serpents are seethed. The supreme symbol of the tunnel is the goddess Qatesh who is seen in vision (by its Adepts) as a radiantly beautiful, naked, woman mounted upon a lion. In her right hand she holds flowers, in her left a serpent. A full moon resting in a crescent is the form of her head-dress. These symbols indicate the lunar current in its active phase. The occult use of the serpent's tongue was well known to the ancients and is still applied to the genitals of the priestess to induce trance.

The equation of the 'place of two cherubs' with the Egyptian Khephra is a dubious etymology. The word properly denotes the Hebraic holy of holies. The real etymology of 'mercy seat' relates to union with the highest principle. Spinning a chaotic and inverse parody from all traditional symbolism without the qualification of anything more than a fanciful imagination is the signature of Grant's style, which consists almost entirely of a conjuration of mere words, with all the emptiness of postmodern linguistic obfuscation and sophistry. The real knowledge conveyed is nil; it is no more than 'creative writing' that pretends to be so much more—the pretence itself forming part of the postmodern irony.

---

94 TAMPIOTh, 610.

20. The satanic inversion of the twentieth path is referred to *Yamatu*, the Genius of the Qliphoth.[95] According to Grant,

> His [Yamatu's] number, 131, is the number of Samael, a name of Satan or Set as Guardian of the Threshold. It is also the number of Pan and of Baphomet, the idol adored of the Templars. MKVNIH, meaning 'her foundation or fundament', a symbol of the *kteis*, also adds to 131.

> The astro-glyph of the 20th Path is Virgo, and its threshold is the *kteis* of the Virgin guarded by Samael. Its magical formula is that of 'virile force reserved' i.e. Karezza, which comports a build-up of sexual energy for magical purposes but without final release.

> Immortality in the flesh is one of the aims of the Black Brothers. The idea arose not only from the natural urge to protect the ego from the impact of death, with its consequent disruption of conscious identity, but also from a misinterpretation of the doctrine of the Death Posture exemplified by the Cult of the Mummy in ancient Khem. It is in fact the magic favoured by occultists who habitually haunt the Tunnel of Yamatu.

> Narcissus, the flower ascribed to this tunnel, yields a key to the nature of the formula of sexual magick associated with it, which, in its dark aspects reflects Karezza as a sterile spending of magical force. The Light, or secret seed, concealed within the body suggests the idea of invisibility and this is the magical *siddhi* attributed to this ray, as also is parthenogenesis. The work of the Black Brothers thus belongs naturally in the Tunnel of Yamatu where the seed, spilt in a sterile act, renders the body bereft of light and therefore 'invisible'.

The inimitable style of Grant is such that in two short sentences he can mention the name of an Archangel (or devil), an Egyptian god, a Greek god, an imaginary god and the Order of Knights Templars, which he accuses (falsely) of adoring the imaginary god! We are then expected to believe that all of this, and the following confusion of symbolism, may be explained through an allusion to various sexual practices. What Grant calls the Death Posture has nothing to do with any Egyptian practice but is in fact something he borrowed from the psychic artist Austin Osman Spare and then 'developed', working on his inspiration drawn from watching early films about Dracula—a figure that Grant very much liked to self-identify with.

---

[95] IAMATO, 131.

ב 4

21. The satanic inversion of the twenty-first path is here referred to *Kurgasiax*, the Genius of the Qliphoth.[96] According to Grant,

> The Lord of the Forces of Life [esoteric title of the 10th Tarot key] becomes The Lady of the Forces of Death; she who sends the incubus and the nightmare.

> The Wheel is the sphere containing the Mark of the Beast which is a revolving chakra that activates the forces of the Sphinx, the dog-headed god, and Typhon. In the Tarot, the wheel becomes the Wheel of the Goddess Fortuna who determines the fluctuation of earthly life. The magical *siddhi* associated with this *kala* is Ascendancy, political or otherwise. Hence the ascription to this Ray of the Sceptre as its typical magical weapon. It is noteworthy that Crowley regarded the formula of Gomorrah, which is the key formula of the Tunnel of Kurgasiax, as the feminine version of the formula of Sodom that obtains on the other side of the Tree at this level.

It takes a perverse stretch of the imagination to link the *kalachakra* with Crowley's notions regarding sodomy, which we will not go into here.[97] The sceptre is almost never a symbol of political power, unless the meaning becomes much degraded. The sceptre is properly the traditional symbol of sacerdotal authority. For example, the sceptre and orb are both symbols of the British monarchs, denoting the union of the sacerdotal and temporal power.

ל ♎

22. The satanic inversion of the twenty-second path is referred to *Lafcursiax*, the Genius of the Qliphoth.[98] According to Grant,

> 671 is a number of major importance in the traditional qabalah. It is the number of the Law (ThORA), the Gate (ThROA), the Wheel or Chakra (ThARO), and the Goddess of Love (AThOR, or Hathor). It is also the number of Adonai, the Holy Guardian Angel, spelt in full. These ideas combined adumbrate the formula of this path, for when the chakra of the goddess is subject to the law or rule of 671 (i.e. Lafcursiax), the Gate of the Abyss is thrown open. Adonai is a glyph of the Sun; the word is usually translated as the 'Lord', but beneath the path Adonai becomes Aidoneus which is a form of Had, the Lord of Hell.

---

[96] ChVRGZATz, 315.
[97] See the notes to the inverse path of Capricorn, p. 90.
[98] LAPQORTzITz, 671.

The name Aidoneus means Invisible or Unseen; in the present context, the invisible form of Adonai which may be evoked by the formula of Lafcursiax.

The scales symbolize the constellation of Libra which rules Path 22. Its reflection in the abyss is tilted by Lafcursiax whose tunnel runs oblique to this path. It represents a blasphemy against the 'adjustment' which is the formula of this Path.

The Egyptian deity attributed to Path 22 is Maat, and it is easy to recognize in the tunnel of Lafcursiax the distortion of Maat's symbols: the balance, the feather, the sword, etc. The Cross of Equilibrium is awry and the Scales upset; the 'Ruler of the Balance' has been put down as the Lord of the Abyss opens the gate of the Dark Goddess and brings forth fantastic beings that haunt this tunnel in the form of ravenous birds with the faces of women who snatch away the souls of the living from their mortal clay.

The magical *siddhi* associated with this tunnel is ability to balance upon the treacherous and funambulatory way that leads from the negative to the positive in the realm of creative chaos. In other words, it enables the magician to spin a web across the Abyss, thus constructing a tenuous and perilous bridge between non-being and being.

One may note that the confusions littering the above text from Grant are indeed typical of the demonic aspects of this path. While the term 'non-being' is used in the Sanskrit texts, it is far more than merely a negation of being, and so the term is used 'in a manner of speaking'.

The absurdity consistent throughout the Nightside narrative is that one might somehow contrive, through means of magick, a bridge between the manifest and the unmanifest; for such means can only pertain to the lowest order, which is at the very limits of what can even exist. The kind of 'non-being' alluded to is the inferior inversion of the undifferentiated state or *prakriti*, which is called 'ignorance' in the Vedanta. The consequences could only mean dispersion for the soul that is divided from its integrality.

It might be noted here that Crowley retitled Tarot Atu Justice VIII to 'Adjustment' in his *Book of Thoth*, thus reducing and limiting the meaning through the Cartesian mechanistic notion of Nature. Justice is the complement of Peace, and these both have a relation with the Shekinah and Metatron. 'Adjustment' on the other hand cannot be said to be a complement of Peace—the principle, not understood by Crowley or Grant, is lost altogether.

23. The satanic inversion of the twenty-third path is *Malkunofat*, the Genius of the Qliphoth.[99] According to Grant,

> There is in this number [307] an element of panic terror exemplified in the word ShVA, which means 'to make a noise', 'crash', 'be terrible'. It derives from the Egyptian word *shefi*, signifying 'terror, terrify', 'terrible' or 'demon-like'. It is the root of the name Shiva, the Hindu god of destruction [*sic*].

> The formula of the sigil [of Malkunofat] may be interpreted as the subjection of the womb or woman by Malkunofat for the purpose of acquiring wealth. The Atu corresponding to the Tunnel of Malkunofat is entitled *The Hanged Man*: The Spirit of the Mighty Waters. This implies the light (or gold) in the Depths. This symbolism accords with the magic *siddhi* attributed to Path 23, i.e. the power of skrying.

> Water (i.e. blood) is the element attributed to the 23rd Path. It is this 'nucleus of impurity' [ref. *The Book of Concealed Mystery*] which the Adept gathers about him. The substance thus vilified was the water of life, i.e. blood; and because its manifestation in the female determined the period of negation or non-openness to the male, it was execrated by an all-male régime as detestable, noisesome, and wholly negative. In the New Aeon of Horus, however, the water is the menstruum of manifestation without which the phenomenal universe would be an impossibility. It is the means of incarnation as well as of magical reification, and as such it is the prime substance of all being, which is NOT (Nuit). This mystery is of a mystical order and can be understood only when the nature of the Goddess is fathomed in its fulness.

As previously pointed out, there is no 'New Aeon' other than that existing in the imagination of some persons. However, the present times, which are traditionally symbolised as the Age of Kali Yuga or of Darkness, are not about manifestation but dissolution at the end of time. It may be the case that the work of Grant and others like him has served, if anything, to hasten that dissolution; certainly, the acceleration of the degeneration of the mass of humanity in the present manifestation has taken place with supernatural assistance. However, the part that Grant and Crowley before him played in this is of very minor significance compared to the influence of the neo-spiritualist movement taken as a whole, whether persons are thought of as being on the side of black or white magic. All of it has served to bring about the aforesaid degeneration.

---

99 MALKVNOPAT, 307.

24. The satanic inversion of the twenty-fourth path is here referred to *Niantiel*, the Genius of the Qliphoth.[100] According to Grant,

> The number 160 is that of QIN, the 'nucleus of impurity' mentioned in connection with the previous tunnel. It is also the number of LNSK, 'for a drink offering', which indicates the sacrament associated with the formula of Niantiel. But a lesser or subsidiary formula is implied by the name MNO (160), which means 'to restrain', or 'keep back', implying the technique of Karezza.

> The Lords of Time are represented in the tunnel of Niantiel by the infernal waters of Scorpio which imply the alchemical formula of purification via putrefaction. The 'infernal waters' are the 'nucleus of impurity' already explained. They suggest the symbolism of the rainbow as the seal of the deluge from the abyss of space.

> The number 160 is that of TzLM, 'an image'. It is an image of death because the water of purification is the blood that negates life in manifestation, while at the same time affirming it in the Abyss where the blood is sucked in as a 'drink offering'.

> The animals prowling in the shadows of this tunnel include the wolf and—as Crowley notes apropos the 24th Path—'the hound as a kind of wolf also pertains here'. This is the hound Cerberus who guards the Abyss. Also ascribed to this 24th *kala* are the scorpion and the beetle, both symbols of the Dark Sun.

> The god-forms appropriate are Typhon, Apep, Khephra, the Merti Goddesses, and Sekhet, the sun of sexual heat, the 'savage' sun in the south as opposed to the great Cat-headed Goddess, Bast, the 'gentle mother' of the north.

> In the Zos Kia Cultus of Austin O. Spare, the adept in this tunnel assumes the 'death posture' and becomes one with cosmic consciousness by a retroversion of the senses. The tantric adept achieves a similar result by the formula of *viparita* described in the Typhonian Trilogy.

> Necrophilia also belongs here as that aspect of meditation on Dissolution that leads the adept to the portal of the Ultimate Mystery of Non-Being. The specifically sexual nature of the formula is made apparent in the attribution to this tunnel of the energies of Scorpio which rule the genital chakras.

---

[100] NIANTIL, 160.

Grant went so far into the mysteries of the Qliphoth of Scorpio that he, perhaps unwittingly, conveyed the demonic traits through his own writing. This includes an investigation of what he has sometimes termed as 'magical practices of the Atlanteans of the Black Temple', for example, which is total fantasy, and based moreover on the fantasies of others. His idea here is that this involves sexual magick combined with necrophilia and the creation of zombies, so effectively superimposing his personal preoccupations on to such fragments of arcane knowledge as he had gathered from diverse (and unreliable) sources. Such zombies are not physical monsters as is portrayed in horror films but elementars that inhabit the lowest, most inferior regions of the subtle or astral plane. These are the remnants of what were were once human souls, prolonged artificially and enslaved by a black magician. Grant notes that such 'Atlantean' forms of magick were 'aimed at incarnating extraterrestrial entities'. In fact, what he describes is a very modern kind of black magic—as modern as his own invention!

It is perhaps needless to add that the 'retroversion of the senses' described here, let alone necrophilia in any shape or form, could not in any way act even as a support to 'cosmic consciousness', since the senses belong wholly to the corporeal human state. The 'Ultimate Mystery of Non-Being' as it is termed here could not be any more than the death and irreversible absorption of the so-called adept in the ignorance of the undifferentiated *prakriti*. What is impressive is the ability of Grant to make something completely ordinary sound as though it were some kind of supreme accomplishment.

$$☾ ♐$$

25. The satanic inversion of the twenty-fifth path is here referred to *Saksaksalim*, Genius of the Qliphoth.[101] According to Grant,

> 300 is the number of Shin, the letter of Spirit. It is the triple fire-tongue symbolic of Chozzar [the sign of Neptune], the disintegrating principle of antimatter. AVR BPAHH (Khabs Am Pekht, Light In Extension) also has this number. It is the False Light, the Great Lie, which is the Word of Choronzon mirrored in the Abyss. Hence, KPhR, 300, is a substance used for covering with pitch or ashes. It derives from the Egyptian word Khepr, 'to transform', 'reverse', or 'regenerate the dead'. The dead are the swathed or bound mummies, and SMR means 'horror', 'as if bound with fear', 'horripilation' (see Job. IV. 15), from the Egyptian *smar*, 'to bind or enswathe for slaughter'.

---

[101] SKSKSLIM, 300.

The concepts of reversal, transformation, and annihilation are also implied. Nephthys is the reifier or transmitter of perfection; the art of transforming raw (i.e. virgin) nature into the image of fulfilment or motherhood.

In the African pantheon, Aidowedo—the rainbow goddess—is the cognate deity. Her coming is likened to the lightning-flash. This is the Sagittarian influence manifesting in the form of the female current. Her fetish is a large serpent that appears only when it wants to drink. It then rests its tail on the ground and thrusts its mouth into the water. It is said that 'he who finds the excrement of this serpent is rich forever.'

'Anti-matter', however, is not any kind of true principle but is merely a modern scientific theory. The notion of 're-generating the dead' rests on impossibility. Grant's assertion, a favourite one with him, that 'Light in Extension' is demonic or infernal, rests on the total inversion of symbolism; this refers in fact to the first manifestation from the supreme principle, which is Pure Being. As such, it is the producer of all manifested being but does not in itself partake of it. The rest of the text involves such confusion that it defies comment other than to say that, as usual, everything is reduced to some form of sexual practice.

עי גּ

26. The satanic inversion of the twenty-sixth path is here referred to *A'ano'nin*, the Genius of the Qliphoth.[102] According to Grant,

> The 22 Paths are reflections in human consciousness of the power zones of cosmic consciousness [the 10 sephiroth]. The aeons may also be considered in relation to the cerebral centres in man, and the *kalas* in relation to the sexual centres. The psychosexual mechanism of the 16 *kalas* in humanity (8 in the female; 8 in the male) is reflected from the aeonic centres or cosmic power zones into the cerebro-spinal fluid and endocrine system.

> The Goat is the astro-glyph of the Scarlet Woman whose EYE (*Ayin*) is attributed to this path via the symbolism of Atu XV, The Devil. This *ain*, or eye, reaches its fullest extent in the name of the Sentinel of this tunnel, i.e. A'ano'nin. His number is 237 which is also that of Ur-He-Ka, the Magick Power of the Goddess ShPhChH (Sefekh), 393.

---

[102] ONVANIN, 237.

237 is also the number of AIREOMAI, 'to be a priest or priestess', which confirms the sacred nature of this number. The magical powers of Path 26 relate to the Witches' Sabbath and the Evil Eye, and its *kala* is that which is distilled by the rite of the XI° for the Evil Eye is the Eye of the Night (i.e. the moon), and the ointment, unguent, or myrrh-dropping is the Vinum Sabbati prepared at sundown in the cauldron of the Scarlet Woman. Capricorn is the Secret Flame whereon the cauldron seethes, hence its connection with Vesta, who, together with the deities Khem, Set, Pan, and Priapus, is assigned to Path 26.

The tunnel of A'ano'nin is haunted by satyrs, fauns, and panic demons, and the Order of Qliphoth is the Dagdagiron, meaning 'the Fishy', which denotes the feminine nature ... the lunar current is the menstruum of reification which seethes within the Cup of Babalon.

There is little in the above other than an inversion of symbolism so that it always points to some form of sexual act. When Grant refers to the XI° (OTO) he means sexual magick of priest and priestess, which confuses menstrual blood with the alchemical Elixir Rubeus or 'red tincture'. This he supposes to be used for 'reification' or obtaining a manifest result. That was Grant's version of the XI° OTO, whereas Crowley, who created the degree system, regarded this as exclusively concerned with homosexual sodomy. Crowley, who slyly depicted the act on his Tarot design for the Devil XV, regarded this as 'superior' to all else. This should convey a clear idea of what Crowley meant by the word 'initiation', especially as the XI° was (and is) the highest in his Order, one step beyond the loftiest administration level X°.[103]

 פ ♂

27. The satanic inversion of the twenty-seventh path is here referred to *Parfaxitas*, the Genius of the Qliphoth.[104] According to Grant,

450 is the number of ThN, meaning 'Dragon'. It is the root of Leviathan. Tan, feminine Tanith, is that great dragon of the deep that manifests on earth as Babalon, the woman or priestess specially consecrated to the work of the Draconian Current.

The formula of Parfaxitas comports the assumption of astral animal forms for the reification of atavistic energies. Some magicians wear an actual mask throughout the rite in order that the astral assumption may gain substance thereby, but this is a matter of personal preference.

---

[103] Crowley considered the number eleven (11) as representing the two male members involved in what he thought of as 'holy initiation'.
[104] PRVHTzTS, 450.

At the moment of the seed's emission the god-form is projected beyond the aura of the magician and nourished by his energy. It then reifies on the astral and sometimes on the etheric plane, where it unites sexually with a similar entity projected by a priestess working the same rite. A successful working is understandably rare, but in cases where the entites attain an objective existence, the result of their congress is such that a very powerful vortex of energy is generated at astral levels of consciousness. It then becomes possible to suck into this vortex the superhuman energies of primal atavisms.

The tunnel of Parfaxitas is littered with the hybrid creatures resulting from imperfectly performed operations of this nature. The animals traditionally associated with this ray are the Owl and the Wolf, hence *Le Mystere Lycanthropique*. Furies and Werewolves haunt its shadows, and the Sword is the magical weapon associated with the deities Mentu, Mars, and Horus the 'flaming God' who rages 'through the firmament with his fantastic spear'. [Ref: *Liber Liberi vel Lapidus Lazuli, VII: 3*, Aleister Crowley]

No comment is required other than to mention that Grant's works are not only more or less pure fiction but were also composed with a sort of malignant glee. He used the terms familiar to occultists so as to ensnare them in the lurid hell of his horrible imaginings.

ש ♈

28. The satanic inversion of the twenty-eighth path is *Tzuflifu*, the Genius of the Qliphoth.[105] According to Grant,

302 is the number of BQR, 'to cut open', 'inquire into', 'dawn', 'dawning of light'. Its anagram, BRQ means 'to lighten', 'send lightning', as applied to the Great Serpent (of the Gnostics). A further metathesis, QBR, signifies 'a cave', 'hole in the earth', 'tomb'. These three letters therefore constitute the type-name of a place of divination founded on the oracle of the womb.

The Atu pertaining to Path 28 is that of *The Emperor*, who is also called 'Sun of the Morning and Chief among the Mighty'. In the Tunnel of Tzuflifu this dawn assumes an almost deliquescent state of heat that resembles a fluid fire-ball. The demons which haunt the tunnel are the furies born of the blood of Uranus who was castrated for crimes against the 'ties of kinship'. The furies (or Erinyes) are depicted in Greek myth as winged women girt with snakes, thus revealing their affinity with the lunar current.

---

[105] TzVPLIPV, 302.

Grant remarks here that the demons of the path are of a Uranian nature corresponding to Da'ath. It thus represents what he terms 'reversion to the source of Non-Being', so that incest is a vice peculiar to this Tunnel of Set. However, Grant either omitted deliberately, or did not know or understand the fact that the universe has both an essential and a substantial pole. The chaos or undifferentiated state of non-being can refer to either pole, depending on the context or point of view, but whereas the essential unmanifest is a real return to the principial source, the absorption in the *prakriti* of the substantial or base end of manifestation is no other than regression to the *sub-infra* and so sub-human states of being. This was a serious omission, especially for those so deluded as to take Grant seriously and put the fantastical conjurations into practice.

Note that Grant here copies the error of Crowley's 'acquired work' of *Liber 777*, and gives the title of the *Emperor IV* as 'Sun of the Morning' instead of *Son* of the Morning; the allusion (book of Isaiah 14: 12) is to Lucifer as the 'son of the morning', which is Venus as the Morning Star, symbol of light and renewal. Thus Christ Jesus is also afforded this title. Through inversion, it becomes the sin of pride, vanity, etc.

ק ♓

29. The satanic inversion of the twenty-ninth path is *Qulielfi,* the Genius of the Qliphoth.[106] According to Grant,

> Tunnel 29 is under the influence of the moon and is the haunt of the witch typified by Hekt, the frog-headed goddess and Lady of Transformation.
>
> The magical power attributed to this 29th *kala* is that of Casting Illusions and Bewitchments generally. The title of the tarot trump ascribed to Path 29 is *The Moon*, its alternative title being the 'Ruler of Flux and Reflux', and the magic mirror is the sole item of equipment in the lunar temple when Qulielfi is evoked. The mirror denotes the crepuscular state of consciousness peculiar to some regions of the astral plane. It is in this state that successful astral working is achieved, for at the borderland of sleep and waking are the 'liers in wait', those elementals that assist in the reification of the inherent dream.

---

[106] QVLILPI, 266.

This tunnel is under the sign of the Frog, the transformer from the waters. This totem typifies the evolution of consciousness from the amphibious to the terrestrial state. The symbolism of the leaper typified by Hekt, the frog-headed goddess of the voltigeurs of the backward paths, is emphasized by the ascription to this *kala* 29 of the Mangrove, the swamp-tree haunted by frogs and other members of the batrachia. Lovecraft has alluded to these creatures as those that foregather in the proximity of the Great Old Ones or their minions. Their croakings herald the emergence from Universe 'B' of the Forces of 'evil' which are—more precisely speaking—the true powers of darkness, or non-being. The mangrove is thus the Tree of Death typical of the 'other side' of the Tree of Life.

As we have previously pointed out, the 'non-being' that is alluded to by Grant across all his works, and with monotonous frequency, can only mean the inferior undifferentiated state called 'ignorance' in the Vedanta. The 'croakings' of those gathering in the proximity of the inverse shadow of the Great Old Ones are similarly an inversion of the Sanskrit *paravak* or primal utterance beyond speech—but in the case of the inversion, it can only indicate the incoherence and disorder inherent in a soul undergoing the dispersion of the 'second death' from which there is no return.

ר ☉

30. The satanic inversion of the thirtieth path is referred to *Raflifu*, the Genius of the Qliphoth.[107] According to Grant,

The *kala* filtering through this tunnel is of a solar nature. In the infernal tube of Raflifu this becomes blackened rather like a deep shadow cast in bright sunlight. The number of Raflifu, 406, is that of the letter Tau spelt in full, or 'extended'. The mystical Tau, or Sign of the Cross, became an emblem of the god of the dead because the Cross symbolizes the crossing over from being to non-being. It is the special emblem of Shaitan, the Chaldean form of Set.

406 is the number of the Hebrew word AThH, meaning 'thou' as in *Do what thou wilt* in the Cult of Thelema. 'Do what thou wilt' is an exhortation to the sun or spirit in the blackness of Amenta, i.e. the subconsciousness. It is an invocation of the True Will and of that spontaneity which is the supreme state of consciousness described by Wei Wu Wei as 'non-volitional living'.

---

[107] RPLIPV, 406.

The leopard is the animal sacred to this tunnel. The black and gold of its spots symbolize the sun in the darkness of Amenta; or, in magical terms, the sexual gold illluminating the subconsciousness with its lightnings. The hawk is the bird of the sun, golden in the upper air where it typifies Horus, black in the abyss where it typifies Set.

The disease typical of this *kala* of solar energy is depletion. The fetors of swamps and marshes are symbolic of the 'sick' sun in Amenta. The qliphoth therefore haunt this tunnel in the form of will o' the wisps or marsh gases that resemble the curious phosphorescences observed by sensitives over the graves of the dead.

Once again we have the usual nonsense of 'crossing over from being to non-being', which only means in this context a descent of the foolish sorcerer to the inferior undifferentiated state. This would certainly result in the 'depletion' that Grant mentions. The second paragraph quoted shows an astonishingly bold corruption of the Chinese tradition; Grant here confuses the 'non-volitional' state with mere immersion in a 'subconsciousness', at the same time reducing the Taoist *action through non-action* to ordinary 'spontaneity'. The non-volitional state, referred to here somewhat incorrectly as 'non-volitional living', is identical to the Hindu *dharmamegha samadhi*, the supreme attainment of full liberation (*moksha*) while still living in the flesh. It certainly does equate to 'Do what thou wilt' in the highest sense, but here Grant reduces all of this to the lowest and most inferior states imaginable.

ש △⊛

31. The satanic inversion of the thirty-first path is referred to *Shalicu*, the Genius of the Qliphoth.[108] According to Grant,

The triple tongue of flame (*shin*) is attributed to Path 31, and this is reflected into the abyss in the form of the inverted trident of Chozzar (a form of Choronzon and an emblem of Atlantean magick). This is the path of Evocation and Pyromancy via the secret fire-tongue that manifests in the tunnel of Shalicu in the form of Choronzon.

Shalicu is the prince of the qliphoth in his form of the arch-devil Choronzon who reigns within this tunnel and who conveys the most secret *kala*, which is known as *The Aeon*. This *kala* flows from the power-zone of Mercury to that of the earth. This tunnel is therefore of prime importance in that it extends to earth the Choronzonic vibrations of Daath, via Mercury.

---

[108] ShOLIKO, 500.

The denizens of this tunnel are the ravenous beasts of the Desert of Set, and they repulse all efforts to gain access to the pylon of Daath. The fire of this path is the fire of Set which is the sexual heat typified by the beasts that lurk on the threshold of Daath before the Veil of the Abyss. The Pyre or Pyramid, and the Fire, are identical; hence the pyramid as a symbol of Set and of the Star Sothis.

The idea of judgement, implicit in the old aeon cults, denotes the purgation and refinement of the gross body (the mummy) and its preparation for the crossing over to Amenta. This is adumbrated in the alchemical formula of the Black Dragon which symbolizes the appearance of the First Matter (Being) in its corrupt or unregenerate state (ego), prior to its projection as the Ultimate Kala (medicine).

The magical *siddhi* of Path 31 is Transformation, Invisibility, or Disappearance; the disappearance of the world of appearances (i.e. the noumenalisation of phenomena which, interpreted in terms of objective existence, is the transformation of the gross body into its ethereal essence).

It is unlikely that the Atlantean tradition had need of such magick as envisioned by Grant, as such applications of traditional sciences are particular to the present Age of Kali Yuga, which reaches back only as far as 6,000 years ago (approximately). However, it is true that the wild boar is a symbol of the primordial tradition, even before that of Atlantis.

The 'Choronzonic vibrations of Da'ath' can mean nothing more than the chaos and madness of the human mind when dispersed and reduced to its elements through the perpetual ignorance of spiritual realities, as expressed through all of Grant's Nightside narratives.

ת ל ▽

32. The satanic inversion of the thirty-second path is here referred to *Thantifaxath*, the Genius of the Qliphoth.[109] According to Grant,

1040 is the number of the Temenos (the precinct of a temple), and of Choros, which, according to *The Canon* (p. 195) was a 'dance by which the earliest worshippers invoked the deity, moving with measured steps around the altar'. In this *kala* are resumed the entire range of macro and microcosmic *kalas*. Sixteen *kalas* are alloted to the macrocosm, and sixteen to the microcosm. The 32nd *kala* pertains to Earth, typified by the altar.

---

[109] ThNTIPATzTh, 1,040.

The magical *siddhis* of this *kala* comprise works of Malediction and Death, and the sickle of Saturn—The Great One of the Night of Time—is the supreme emblem of this Tunnel which is the resort of ghouls and larvae of the pit lit by the lurid phosphorescent glare of corpse candles. The Ash and Cypress, the Nightshade, the Elm, and the Yew, are the trees of darkness in whose shadows the tunnel disappears into the deepest cells of the earth. Yet this tunnel has affinities with the ocean of space through its association with Set, the child of the Goddess of the Seven Stars whose planetary vehicle is Saturn.

Sebek, the crocodile, is the zöomorphic emblem of this tunnel, and Mako—a name of Set as the son of Typhon and the powers of darkness— is the secret deity of this nethermost cell. The God Terminus also belongs here, for this outpost of the cosmic system is truly the end of the cosmic vibrations which, from this point, return to their source in the stars. The works of this tunnel include incarceration or 'tying up as a corpse' in the swathings of eternity.

The 32nd [path] transmits the astral energies of Yesod to the sphere of Malkuth thereby effecting the final 'earthing' of all the *kalas* and influences that have streamed through the tunnels from Pluto (Kether) to Earth (Malkuth). But at this utmost and final earthing of the cosmic current a sudden reversal occurs; and this is the formula of Magick itself, that the Current having earthed itself in Malkuth now turns back upon itself and streaks up the Tree to dissolve in its source in the transcosmic centres of energy represented by Kether. Thus 'Malkuth is in Kether and Kether is in Malkuth', though after a different manner.

The allusion to 'astral energies' in the last paragraph quoted typifies the vague and almost completely meaningless invention and use of terms by Theosophists and other neo-spiritualists, based on popular scientism. The attribution of outer planets to the supernal sephiroth, as with Pluto to Kether, separates the Tree from any true principle— the supernals are not within the cosmological domain. As a hellish inversion, the attribution works, but Grant is here using it to cheat us with a diabolical confusion, substituting 'transcosmic' for the dark realm of Tartarus, below the earth. In Eternity, there can be no 'tying up a corpse'; Eternity is not subject to either birth or death. What he calls 'transcosmic centres of energy' is thus the *sub-infra* level *below* that of manifestation and not beyond it. When a current is 'earthed' it stops there. Given that the schema here is an inversion, then if the current could return to Kether it would only be following the same downward trajectory and the dissolution is then that of the wholly negative destruction of the soul—we are back in Tartarus. Anyone following such advice as is given by Grant here would undoubtedly meet the 'God Terminus', and that is indeed as far as it goes.

Tunnels of Set: Conclusions

The danger of presenting a work such as the foregoing is that it may seem to place undue significance on one person. Though Kenneth Grant undoubtedly exerted influence on postmodern occultism, such an influence, as with that of Crowley before him, is negligible compared to the devastation wrought by neo-spiritualism as propagated by the Theosophical movement.[110] There will no doubt be some, limited by an egoistic view of all things, that will accuse us of having some axe to grind with Grant personally. However, while Grant's writings were 'diabolical' in nature, something he would not have disagreed with and would probably find flattering, none of this is to suggest that the man was personally 'evil'. All those who knew him found him charming and personable. It is only necessary to say this as we live in times when people are far more interested in the 'personalities' than the work of those personalities.

It must also be said that we are in no way singling out a particular school or section of occultism as deviant and destructive to those who might otherwise stand a chance of making spiritual progress. There is a 'white magic' school that has always condemned the works of Crowley and Grant, but unfortunately for the wrong reasons! This, sometimes calling itself the 'Right hand path' as opposed to the 'Left hand path' (neither of these designations is in any way correct), rests on an entirely false and distorted knowledge culled from diverse sources, much of it owing to psychism, and as in the case of the very influential Theosophical movement, whose propaganda underpins much of its notions, fake psychism at that. A mere glance through the pages of *Magic and the Magician*, W.E. Butler, for one example, reveals the word 'power' or 'energy' appearing a dozen times on each page. It is as though the sole purpose of it all is to 'raise power', and from very inferior sources, often explained as 'collective mind' or by some other psychological term. Let it be clear then, that there is little to choose between 'black' and 'white' schools of magic. In reality, they might as well all be in the same boat enjoying the same hellish cocktail party. The fact they throw mud at each other owes to the nature of their communion cup, filled with a toxic elixir drawn from scientism, 'evolution', 'progress' and psychological theories.

---

[110] See René Guénon, *Theosophy: History of a Pseudo-Religion.*

97

As a final word, to address the question as to why we have even bothered to append to an otherwise serious book on the Qabalah what amounts to a comic strip parody of the occult, we will provide a quotation here from René Guénon, who was crystal clear on all such matters. We should not in any way underestimate the scale of the influence of neo-spiritualism and its practices on our environment, even the cosmological environment. In 'The Fissures in the Great Wall', Guénon explains how the materialisation of our world reached its apotheosis some time ago, and that ever since then we have been heading not towards more and more materialism but towards the final (and actual) dissolution of the world.[111]

'Fissures' have been mentioned previously as being the paths whereby certain destructive forces are already entering, and must continue to enter more freely; according to traditional symbolism these fissures occur in a Great Wall that surrounds the world and protects it from the intrusion of malefic influences coming from the inferior subtle domain. In order that this symbolism may be fully understood in all its aspects, it is important to note that a wall acts both as a protection and as a limitation: in a sense therefore it can be said to have both advantages and inconveniences; but insofar as its principal purpose is to ensure an adequate defence against attacks coming from below, the advantages are incomparably the more important, for it is on the whole more useful to anyone who happens to be enclosed within its perimeter to be kept out of reach of what is below, than it is to be continuously exposed to the ravages of the enemy, or worse still to more or less complete destruction. In any case, a walled space as such is not closed in at the top, so that communication with superior domains is not prevented, and this state of affairs is the normal one; but in the modern period the 'shell' with no outlet built by materialism has cut off that communication. Moreover, as already explained, because the 'descent' has not yet come to an end, the shell must necessarily remain intact overhead, that is, in the direction of that from which humanity need not be protected since on the contrary only beneficent forces can come that way; the fissures occur only at the base, and therefore the actual protective wall itself, and the inferior forces that make their way through them meet with a much reduced resistance because under such conditions no power of a superior order can intervene in order to oppose them effectively. Thus the world is exposed defenceless to all the attacks of its enemies, the more so because, the present day mentality being what it is, the dangers that threaten it are wholly unperceived.

---

[111] René Guénon, *The Reign of Quantity and the Signs of the Times*.

Appendices i

The Sentinels of the Tunnels of Set

Tunnel	Guardian	Name	Value
11.	AMPRVDIS	Amprodias	401
12.	BRTChIL	Baratchial	260
13.	QRGGPZ	Gargophias	393
14.	DGDGIAL	Dagdagiel	55
15.	HMThTRTh	Hemethterith	1054
16.	ORIHNS	Oriens	395
17.	ZAMRDIL	Zamradiel	292
18.	ChARAKITh	Characith	640
19.	TAMPIOTh	Temphioth	610
20.	IAMATO	Yamatu	131
21.	ChVRGZATz	Kurgasix	315
22.	LAPQORTzITz	Lafcursiax	671
23.	MALKVNOPAT	Malkunofat	307
24.	NIANTIL	Niantiel	160
25.	SKSKSLIM	Saksaksalim	300
26.	ONVANIN	A'ano'nin	237
27.	PRVHTzTS	Parfaxitas	450
28.	TzVPLIPV	Tzuflifu	302
29.	QVLILPI	Qulielfi	266
	or QVLPI		226
30.	RPLIPV	Raflifu	406
31.	ShOLIKO	Shalicu	500
32.	ThNTIPATzTh	Thantifaxath	1040

Appendices ii

Key Scale Correspondences

Hebrew Letter Values

☩	Letter	Meaning	Figure	Value		English
11.	Aleph	Ox	א	1		A
12.	Beth	House; tent	ב	2		B
13.	Gimel	Camel; tether	ג	3		G
14.	Daleth	Door; bolt	ד	4		D
15.	Hé	Window	ה	5		H, E
16.	Vav	Pin; nail	ו	6		V, U
17.	Zain	Sword	ז	7		Z
18.	Cheth	Fence; enclosure	ח	8		Ch
19.	Teth	Serpent	ט	9		T
20.	Yod	Hand	י	10		I, J or Y
21.	Kaph	Palm of hand	כ ך	20	500	K
22.	Lamed	Scourge [Sickle]	ל	30		L
23.	Mem	Water	מ ם	40	600	M
24.	Nun	Fish	נ ן	50	700	N
25.	Samekh	Tent prop	ס	60		S
26.	Ayin	Eye	ע	70		O, A'a
27.	Pé	Mouth	פ ף	80	800	P
28.	Tzaddi	Fish-hook	צ ץ	90	900	Tz
29.	Qoph	Skull	ק	100		Q
30.	Resh	Head	ר	200		R
31.	Shin	Tooth	ש	300		S, Sh
32.	Tav	Cross; mark; way	ת	400		T, Th

✠	Sephira	Translation	Hebrew
1.	Kether	Crown	KThR
2.	Chokmah	Wisdom	ChKMH
3.	Binah	Understanding	BINH
4.	Chesed; Gedulah	Love; Magnificence	ChSD; GDVLH
5.	Geburah	Strength	GBVRH
6.	Tiphereth	Beauty	ThPARTh
7.	Netzach	Victory	NTzCh
8.	Hod	Splendour	HVD
9.	Yesod	Foundation	YSVD
10.	Malkuth	Kingdom	MLKVTh
11.	Da'ath	Knowledge	DOTh

✠	Gods of Atziluth	Translation	Hebrew, Greek
1.	Asherah	Holy One	AShRH
2.	IAO	The Immortal	IAΩ
3.	Elohim	Gods (male-female)	ALHIM
4.	El	Lord	AL
5.	Elohim Gibor	Mighty Gods	ALHIM GBVR
6.	Iao Eloah ve-Da'ath	God of Knowledge	IAΩ ALVH V-DOTh
7.	Iao Tzabaoth	Lord of Hosts	IAΩ TzBAVTh
8.	Elohim Tzabaoth	God of Hosts	ALHIM TzBAVTh
9.	Shaddai El Chai	God of Life	ShDI AL ChI
10.	Adonai, Adonath	Lord, Lady of Earth	ADNI V-ADNTh
11.	Iao Elohim	Immortal Gods	IAΩ ALHIM

✝	Archangels of Briah	Translation	Hebrew, Greek
1.	Metatron	Beyond	MTTRVN
2.	Ratziel	Will	RTzIAL
3.	Tzaphqiel	Seer	TzPQIAL
4.	Tzadqiel	Holy	TzDQIAL
5.	Kamael	Flame	KMAL
6.	Raphael	Curator	RPAL
7.	Auriel	Light	AVRIAL
8.	Michael	Strong	MIKAL
9.	Gabriel	Mighty	GBRIAL
10.	Sandalphon	Lover; Helper	SNDLPVN
11.	ISAIST	Justice	ΙΣΑΙΣΤ

✝	Angels of Yetzirah	Translation	Hebrew
1.	Chaioth Ha-Chadesh	Holy Living Creatures	ChIVTh H-ChDSh
2.	Auphanim	Wheels	AVPNIM
3.	Aralim	Thrones	ARALIM
4.	Chashmalim	Shining Ones	ChShMLIM
5.	Seraphim	Fiery Serpents	ShRPIM
6.	Malachim	Kings	MLKIM
7.	Elohim	Gods	ALHIM
8.	Beni Elohim	Sons of Gods	BNI ALHIM
9.	Kerubim	The Strong	KRVBIM
10.	Ashim	Souls of Fire	AShIM
11.	Seraphim	Flying Serpents	ShRPIM

✠	Chakras	Translation		Hebrew
1.	Rashith Ha-Gilgalim	Swirling Force (Primum Mobile)		RAShITh H-GLGLIM
2.	Mazloth	Zodiac		MSLVTh
3.	Shabathai	Saturn	Rest	ShBThAI
4.	Tzedek	Jupiter	Virtue	TzDQ
5.	Madim	Mars	Strength	MADIM
6.	Shemesh	Sun	Light	ShMSh
7.	Nogah	Venus	Splendour	NVGH
8.	Kokab	Mercury	Starlight	KVKB
9.	Levanah	Moon	Lunar Flame	LBNH
10.	Cholem Yesodeth	Elements	Earth	ChLM ISVDVTh
11.	AUM	Knowledge		DOTh

The Scales of Colour

There are four worlds of the Qabalah.

ש Atziluth; Emanations; Gods

ב Briah; Creation; Archangels

א Yetzirah; Formation; Orders of Angels

ה Assiah; Material Universe; Elements

There is a scale of colour for each. For general purposes:

The sephiroth are imaged in the Queen scale.

The connecting paths are imaged in the King scale.

This produces a balanced Tree of Life for meditation.

The first 10 numbers are the sephiroth. Numbers 11–32 are the connecting paths. Number 33 is Da'ath.

☩	King Scale (Atziluth)	Queen Scale (Briah)
1.	Brilliance	White brilliance
2.	Pure soft blue	Silvery light
3.	Crimson	Black
4.	Deep violet	Blue
5.	Orange	Scarlet
6.	Clear pink rose	Yellow-gold
7.	Amber	Emerald
8.	Blue-violet	Orange
9.	Indigo	Violet
10.	Yellow	Citrine, olive, russet, black
11.	Bright pale yellow	Sky blue
12.	Yellow	Purple
13.	Blue	Silver
14.	Emerald	Sky blue
15.	Violet	Sky blue
16.	Red-orange	Deep indigo
17.	Orange	Pale violet
18.	Amber	Maroon
19.	Yellow-green	Deep purple
20.	Green-yellow	Slate grey
21.	Violet	Blue
22.	Emerald	Blue
23.	Deep blue	Sea-green
24.	Green-blue	Dark reddish brown
25.	Blue	Yellow
26.	Indigo	Black
27.	Scarlet	Red
28.	Scarlet	Red
29.	Crimson or ultraviolet	Buff, flecked silvery white
30.	Orange	Gold yellow
31. △	Bright orange-scarlet	Vermillion
31. ✷	Silver	Dark akasha purple (nearly black)
32. ♄	Indigo	Black
32. ▽	Dark green or olive	Amber
33.	Blue-violet	Silver

⊕	Prince Scale (Yetzirah)	Princess Scale (Assiah)
1.	White brilliance	White, flecked gold
2.	Mother-of-pearl	White flecked red, blue, yellow
3.	Deep scarlet	Silver, rayed cerise
4.	Deep purple	Deep azure, flecked yellow
5.	Bright scarlet	Red, flecked black
6.	Rich salmon (cerise)	Gold amber
7.	Bright yellow green	Olive, flecked gold
8.	Red-russet	Yellowish brown flecked white
9.	Very dark purple	Citrine, flecked azure
10.	As Queen Scale, flecked gold	Black, rayed yellow
11.	Blue emerald green	Emerald, flecked gold
12.	Grey	Indigo, rayed violet
13.	Cold pale blue	Silver, rayed sky blue
14.	Spring green	Bright rose, rayed pale green
15.	Bluish mauve	White, tinged purple
16.	Deep warm olive	Rich brown
17.	New yellow leather	Reddish grey, inclined to mauve
18.	Rich bright russet	Dark greenish brown
19.	Silvery grey	Reddish amber
20.	Greenish grey	Plum
21.	Rich purple	Bright blue, rayed yellow
22.	Deep blue green	Pale green
23.	Deep olive-green	Mother-of-pearl
24.	Very dark brown	Livid indigo or black beetle-brown
25.	Green	Dark vivid blue
26.	Blue-black	Cold dark grey, near black
27.	Venetian red	Bright red rayed azure or emerald
28.	Brilliant flame	Glowing red
29.	Light translucent cerise	Stone
30.	Rich amber	Amber, rayed red
31. △	Scarlet, rayed gold	Vermillion rayed crimson, emerald
31. ⊕	Prism, with violet outside	White, red, yellow, blue, black
32. ♄	Blue black	Black, rayed blue
32. ▽	Beetle black	Black, rayed yellow
33.	Violet	Silvery gold

☩	Letter		Symbol		Tarot Atu
11.	א	Aleph	△		The Fool 0
12.	ב	Beth	☿		The Magician I
13.	ג	Gimel	☽		The Priestess II
14.	ד	Daleth	♀		The Empress III
15.	ה	Hé	♒		The Star XVII
16.	ו	Vav	♉		The Hierophant V
17.	ז	Zain	♊		The Lovers VI
18.	ח	Cheth	♋		The Chariot VII
19.	ט	Teth	♌		Strength XI
20.	י	Yod	♍		The Hermit IX
21.	כ	Kaph	♃		The Wheel of Fortune X
22.	ל	Lamed	♎		Justice VIII
23.	מ	Mem	▽		The Hanged Man XII
24.	נ	Nun	♏		Death XIII
25.	ס	Samekh	♐		Temperance XIV
26.	ע	Ayin	♑		The Devil XV
27.	פ	Pé	♂		The Tower (of God) XVI
28.	צ	Tzaddi	♈		The Emperor IV
29.	ק	Qoph	♓		The Moon XVIII
30.	ר	Resh	☉		The Sun XIX
31.	ש	Shin	✹	△	Judgement XX
32.	ת	Tav	♄	▽	The World XXI

Key Scale		Magical Powers
1. Crown		Union with God
2. Wisdom		Vision of God Face to Face
3.	♄	Vision of Sorrow and Trance of Wonder
4.	♃	Vision of Love
5.	♂	Vision of Power
6.	☉	Vision of Harmony (Beatitude); Mysteries of the Rosy Cross
7.	♀	Vision of Beauty Triumphant
8.	☿	Vision of Splendour [Ezekiel]
9.	☽	Vision of the Secret Nature of the Universe
10.	⊕	Vision of the Holy Guardian Angel or of Adonai
11.	△	Divination (especially ROTA)
12.	☿	Miracles; Eloquence; Languages; Knowledge and Sciences
13.	☽	White Eagle (Alchemical Tincture); Clairvoyance; Dreams
14.	♀	Love potions; Charisma
15.	≈	Astrology or Starry Wisdom
16.	♉	Secret of the Ka or Vital Force; Energy of Work
17.	♊	Being in two places at one time; Prophecy
18.	♋	Enchantments; Transformations (as Khephra)
19.	♌	Intelligence of Birds and Animals
20.	♍	Invisibility; Parthenogenesis; Resurrection and Life
21.	♃	Power and influence over others
22.	♎	Works of Justice and Equilibrium
23.	▽	Great Work; Talismans; Crystal-gazing
24.	♏	Necromancy; Resurrection
25.	♐	Transmutations; Universal Peacock or Rainbow
26.	♑	Witches Sabbath and the Evil Eye
27.	♂	Works of Vengeance
28.	♈	Works of Consecration
29.	♓	Bewitchments and Casting Illusions; Magical Memory
30.	☉	Red Eagle (Alchemical Tincture); Acquisition of Wealth
31.	△	Evocation; Pyromancy
	⊛	Raising the Dead; Transformations
32.	♄	Curses
	▽	Talismans; Alchemy; Geomancy; Astral Travel

Key Scale		Weapons of Art
1. Crown		Crown, Filet, Tiara or Nemmys; Lamp; Fylfot Cross
2. Wisdom		Shiva Lingam; Wand; Inner Robe of Glory; *was* sceptre
3.	♄	Yoni; Outer Robe of Concealment; Cup
4.	♃	Wand, Sceptre; *hekat* sceptre; Vajra or Thunderbolt
5.	♂	Sword of Strength, Spear; *nekhakha* sceptre
6.	☉	Lamen; Rosy Cross; Cup for the Mass; Bell; Altar (as heart)
7.	♀	Lamp (of Dadouchos); Thurible; Girdle; *ankh*
8.	☿	Words and Spells; the Name; Cup of Stolistes
9.	☽	The Altar; Perfumes and Sandals; Mirror; Cauldron
10.	⊕	Circle of the Place and Triangle of Evocation
11.	🜁	Dagger or Sword for Air; Feather or Fan
12.	☿	Caduceus Staff; Stylus or Pen
13.	☽	Bow and Arrow (Artemis, Apollo, Neïth)
14.	♀	Girdle; *ankh*; Door or Gate
15.	≈	Censer (Incense); Aspergillum (Lustral Water)
16.	♉	Labour of Preparation; Throne and Altar
17.	♊	Tripod (for incense); Cauldron (oracles)
18.	♋	Graal; Furnace; Scarab
19.	♌	The Discipline of the Work; Phoenix Wand
20.	♍	Lamp and Staff; Cloak; Bread or Cakes
21.	♃	Sceptre; Vajra or Thunderbolt
22.	♎	Cross of Equilibrium; Scales; Sickle or Scythe
23.	🜄	Cup for Water; Wine; Red Cross and White Triangle
24.	♏	Oath and Obligation; Ark and Sektet or Hennu Boat
25.	♐	The Arrow (and Rainbow)
26.	♑	Occult Force; Lamp or Torch; *was* sceptre
27.	♂	Sword of Strength
28.	♈	Horns; Energy (Minerva); Burin
29.	♓	Twilight of the Place and Magical Mirror
30.	☉	Lamen; Zodiac; Bow and Arrow
31.	🜂	Tetrahedron Pyramid; Wand for Fire
	✸	Winged Akashic Egg
32.	♄	Sickle or Scythe
	🜃	Pentacle; Bread and Salt, Silver and Gold

Key Scale		Perfumes
1. Crown		Ambergris
2. Wisdom		Musk
3.	♄	Myrrh
4.	♃	Cedar
5.	♂	Dragon's Blood (and all hot, fiery perfumes)
6.	☉	Frankincense (Olibanum)
7.	♀	Benzoin; Rose; Sandalwood
8.	☿	Storax (as menstruum)
9.	☽	Jasmine; Ginseng and all odiferous roots
10.	⊕	Dittany of Crete
11.	△	Galbanum; Mint
12.	☿	Mastic; White Sandal; Mace; Storax (and all fugitive odours)
13.	☽	Camphor; Aloes (and all sweet feminine perfumes)
14.	♀	Sandalwood; Myrtle (and all soft voluptuous perfumes)
15.	≈	Galbanum; Night-scented Stock (all nocturnal perfumes)
16.	♉	Storax
17.	♊	Wormwood (by association with Absinthe)
18.	♋	Onycha (and all oceanic perfumes)
19.	♌	Olibanum
20.	♍	Narcissus; White Musk
21.	♃	Saffron; Sage (and all generous perfumes)
22.	♎	Galbanum (seduction and treachery); All balanced odours
23.	▽	Myrrh; Onycha (and all oceanic perfumes)
24.	♏	Siamese Benzoin; Opopanax (and all abominable perfumes)
25.	♐	Lignum Aloes; Saffron; Cedarwood
26.	♑	Musk
27.	♂	Dragon's Blood (and all hot, fiery perfumes)
28.	♈	Dragon's Blood (and all hot, fiery perfumes)
29.	♓	Ambergris; Onycha
30.	☉	Frankincense; Cinnamon; Orange
31.	△	Frankincense; all fiery perfumes
	⊛	Natron
32.	♄	Patchouli; Indigo; Storax; Assafoetida
	▽	Sulphur (and all noxious odours)

Key Scale		Precious Stones
1. Crown		Diamond; Star Sapphire
2. Wisdom		Star Ruby; Turquoise
3.	♄	Star Sapphire; Black Diamond; Pearl
4.	♃	Amethyst; Sapphire; Lapis Lazuli
5.	♂	Ruby
6.	☉	Topaz; Yellow Diamond
7.	♀	Emerald
8.	☿	Opal; Fire Opal
9.	☽	Quartz (as Foundation)
10.	⊕	Rock Crystal
11.	△	Topaz; Chalcedony (clouds; air)
12.	☿	Opal; Agate
13.	☽	Moonstone; Pearl; Crystal
14.	♀	Emerald; Turquoise
15.	≈	Crystal; Star Sapphire; Chalcedony (as clouds)
16.	♉	Topaz
17.	♊	Alexandrite; Tourmaline; Iceland Spar (all light polarising)
18.	♋	Amber
19.	♌	Cat's Eye
20.	♍	Peridot
21.	♃	Amethyst; Lapis Lazuli
22.	♎	Emerald
23.	▽	Beryl; Aquamarine
24.	♏	Snakestone; Green Turquoise
25.	♐	Jacinth (Hyacinth)
26.	♑	Black Diamond (as pupil of the eye)
27.	♂	Ruby (and all red stones)
28.	♈	Ruby
29.	♓	Pearl (cloudy luminosity of astral visions)
30.	☉	Crysoleth
31.	△	Fire Opal
	⊛	Black Diamond
32.	♄	Onyx
	⊝	Salt

110

Key Scale		Plants
1. Crown		Almond in flower; Lotus; Banyan (Indian fig)
2. Wisdom		Amaranth (as immortal); Mistletoe
3.	♄	Lotus; Lily; Ivy; Cypress; Opium Poppy
4.	♃	Olive; Shamrock; Poppy
5.	♂	Oak; Hickory; Nux Vomica; Nettle; Gorse
6.	☉	Oak; Ash; Acorn; Acacia; Bay; Laurel (Apollo); Vine (Dionysus)
7.	♀	Rose; Laurel
8.	☿	Moly (Hermes); Anhalonium Lewinii (Peyote)
9.	☽	Jasmine; Banyan; Mandrake; Damiana; Ginseng; Yohimba
10.	+	Willow; Lily; Ivy; Wheat; Corn; Pomegranate
11.	🜁	Aspen
12.	☿	Vervain; Herb Mercury; Marjolaine (Oregano); Palm; Lime; Nuts
13.	☽	Almond; Hazel; Mugwort; Moonwort; Ranunculus (White Water Crow-foot, Buttercup); Pomegranate
14.	♀	Fig; Peach; Apple; Myrtle; Rose; Clover
15.	♒	Olive; Coconut
16.	♉	Mallow; All large or gigantic trees
17.	♊	Orchids (and all hybrids)
18.	♋	Lotus
19.	♌	Sunflower; Marigold
20.	♍	Snowdrop; Lily; Narcissus; Mistletoe
21.	♃	Hyssop; Oak; Poplar; Fig; Arnica; Cedar
22.	♎	Aloe
23.	▽	Lotus; Alder (and all water plants)
24.	♏	Nettle; Cactus (and all spiky or poisonous plants)
25.	♐	Rush (for arrows); Sage
26.	♑	Indian Hemp; Orchis Root; Thistle; Ginseng
27.	♂	Absinthe; Rue
28.	♈	Tiger Lily; Geranium; Olive (Minerva)
29.	♓	Opium; Mangrove; Plankton (and all unicellular organisms)
30.	☉	Sunflower; Marigold; Laurel; Heliotrope; Ginger; Nuts
31.	△ ⊛	Red Poppy; Hibiscus; Nettle Almond in flower
32.	♄ 🜃	Ash; Elm; Cypress; Hellebore; Yew; Nightshade Oak; Ivy; Corn

Key Scale		Birds, Animals and Fabled Creatures
1. Crown		Sphinx; Dragon (as Draco); Hawk; Oryx
2. Wisdom		Unicorn (Oryx); Oyster
3.	♄	Goose; Bee; Corvids; Ass (and all Typhonian Creatures)
4.	♃	Unicorn; Horse; Centaur; Dolphin; Albatross
5.	♂	Basilisk; Shark
6.	☉	Phoenix (Heron, Kite); Lion (and all cats); Pelican; Peacock
7.	♀	Lynx; Cow (as Hathoor); Raven; Bee
8.	☿	Jackal; Rhinoceros; Unicorn; Hermaphrodites
9.	☽	Jackal; Elephant (Ganesha); Frogs and Toads (Hekate)
10.	⊕	Sphinx
11.	△	Owl; Eagle, Hawk; Sylphs
12.	☿	Swallow; Ibis; Ape (of Thoth)
13.	☽	Camel; Owl; Hound (Artemis); Stork; Cats, Bats (etc.)
14.	♀	Swan; Dove; Sparrow
15.	≈	Peacock; Eagle, Hawk; Owl (Ishtar)
16.	♉	Bull
17.	♊	Magpie; Parrot; Zebra; Penguin; Chimera (and all hybrids)
18.	♋	Whale; Crab; Turtle; Scarab
19.	♌	Lion; Tiger; Lion-serpent
20.	♍	All solitary creatures; Cats (and all small furry animals)
21.	♃	Eagle; Albatross (and all large creatures); Praying Mantis
22.	♎	Lion (as Egyptian *ma'a*); Scorpion (Babylonian); Spider
23.	▽	Eagle, Snake, Scorpion; Nymphs (and all aquatic creatures)
24.	♏	Eagle, Snake, Scorpion; Lobster; Crayfish; Wolf; Arachnids
25.	♐	Albatross; Horse; Centaur; Hippogriff
26.	♑	Corvids; Oyster; Goat; Ass; Satyr (all Typhonian Creatures)
27.	♂	Horse; Bear; Wolf
28.	♈	Ram; Owl (Minerva)
29.	♓	Fish; Dolphin; Mermaids; Scarab (Khephra); Jackal
30.	☉	Lion; Leopard; Sparrowhawk
31.	△	Lion; Salamander
	✳	Sphinx
32.	♄	Crocodile
	▽	Bull; Hippopotamus; Dryads

Key Scale		Legendary Orders of Being
11.	△	Sylphs
12.	☿	Witches and Wizards; 'Voices'
13.	☽	Ghosts and Lemures
14.	♀	Succubi
15.	♒	Extraterrestrials
16.	♉	Gorgons; Minotaurs
17.	♊	Banshees; Ominous apparitions; Chimarae
18.	♋	Vampires
19.	♌	Dragons; Horror and dread
20.	♍	Banshees; Cat-faced demons
21.	♃	Giants; Incubi; Nightmares
22.	♎	Fairies; Harpies
23.	▽	Nymphs & Undines; Sirens; Mermaids
24.	♏	Witches; Stryges; Lamiae; Trolls
25.	♐	Centaurs
26.	♑	Satyrs and Fauns; Panic-demons
27.	♂	Furies; Boars
28.	♈	Mania; Erinyes (Furies)
29.	♓	Phantoms; Were-wolves; Dog-faced demons
30.	☉	Will o' the Wisp
31.	△	Salamanders
	✹	Daemons; Genii
32.	♄	Ghouls; Larvae; Corpse Candles
	▽̵	Dweller on the Threshold; Gnomes

☥	Virtues	Vices
3.	Silence	Avarice
4.	Obedience (to the path)	Bigotry, Hypocrisy, Gluttony, Tyranny
5.	Energy and Courage	Cruelty and Destruction
6.	Devotion to the Great Work	Pride and Egotism
7.	Faith; Unselfishness	Unchastity (unfaithful to chosen path)
8.	Truthfulness	Falsehood and Dishonesty
9.	Independence	Idleness
10.	Discrimination	Inertia and Avarice
11.	Perfection of all Virtues	Infantilism and Isolationism

Selected Works of Oliver St. John

Hermetic Astrology (2015)
Magical Theurgy (2015)
The Enterer of the Threshold (2016)
Liber 373 Astrum Draconis (2017)
Hermetic Qabalah Foundation—Complete Course (2018)
Babalon Unveiled! Thelemic Monographs (2019)
Ritual Magick—Initiation of the Star and Snake (2019)
Nu Hermetica—Initiation and Metaphysical Reality (2021)
The Way of Knowledge in the Reign of Antichrist (2022)
Thirty-two paths of Wisdom (2023)
Thunder Perfect Gnosis—Intellectual Flower of Mind (2023)
The Law of Thelema—Hidden Alchemy (2024)
Metamorphosis—Hermetic Science and Yoga Power (2024)
Dreaming Thelema and Magical Art (2024)
Advaita Vedanta—Question of the Real (2025)
Egyptian Tarot and Guide Book (Crossed Crow Books, 2025)

The dates given are of first publication. All works published prior to 2021 have since been extensively revised and new editions produced.

Contact the O∴A∴

Contact details and information is posted on our website:

www.ordoastri.org